Working Globally

Sally Lansdell

- Take the fast track route to a successful international career

- Covers all the key aspects of working globally, from identifying the key managerial competences to dealing with culture shock and trusting your intuition to finding the right information

- Packed with lessons and tips from the global working gurus including Elizabeth Marx, Rowan Gibson and Michael Lissack

- Includes a glossary of key concepts and a comprehensive resources guide

>>EXPRESS EXEC.COM<<
essential management thinking at your fingertips

LIFE & WORK

10.02

Copyright © Capstone Publishing 2002

The right of Sally Lansdell to be identified as the author of this work has been asserted in accordance with the Copyright, Designs and Patents Act 1988

First published 2002 by
Capstone Publishing (a Wiley company)
8 Newtec Place
Magdalen Road
Oxford OX4 1RE
United Kingdom
http://www.capstoneideas.com

CIP catalogue records for this book are available from the British Library and the US Library of Congress

ISBN 1-84112-202-5

This book is printed on acid-free paper

Substantial discounts on bulk quantities of Capstone books are available to corporations, professional associations and other organizations. Please contact Capstone for more details on +44 (0)1865 798 623 or (fax) +44 (0)1865 240 941 or (e-mail) info@wiley-capstone.co.uk

Contents

To Jack, for being there

Introduction to ExpressExec

ExpressExec is 3 million words of the latest management thinking compiled into 10 modules. Each module contains 10 individual titles forming a comprehensive resource of current business practice written by leading practitioners in their field. From brand management to balanced scorecard, ExpressExec enables you to grasp the key concepts behind each subject and implement the theory immediately. Each of the 100 titles is available in print and electronic formats.

Through the ExpressExec.com Website you will discover that you can access the complete resource in a number of ways:

» printed books or e-books;
» e-content – PDF or XML (for licensed syndication) adding value to an intranet or Internet site;
» a corporate e-learning/knowledge management solution providing a cost-effective platform for developing skills and sharing knowledge within an organization;
» bespoke delivery – tailored solutions to solve your need.

Why not visit www.expressexec.com and register for free key management briefings, a monthly newsletter and interactive skills checklists. Share your ideas about ExpressExec and your thoughts about business today.

Please contact elound@wiley-capstone.co.uk for more information.

Introduction

In this chapter we consider examples of global organizations and global culture, to explain the background to working globally. As the world "shrinks," there is more and more need for everyone in business to have international experience.

The world at the beginning of the twenty-first century has become much closer to what Canadian communications theorist Marshall McLuhan called a "global village."[1] Organizations, even small ones, buy, sell, and operate on a global basis; in much of the world there is arguably a global (mainly Americanized) culture; and it is now more possible than ever before for people to work in other countries, in multinational, often dispersed teams, and for customers in other countries without leaving their home base. These are trends that are only set to intensify.

A glance at a week's editions of any broadsheet newspaper will offer many instances of this. Examples from the *Financial Times* are given below.

» As I write, the news is dominated by the terrorist attacks in New York and Washington. Part of what has given this event so much force around the world is the spread of nationalities of those who died working in the World Trade Center. US Secretary of State Colin Powell was reported as saying that 62 nations had lost citizens in the attack.[2]

» International Monetary Fund managing director Horst Kohler commented on the coordinated response of the central banks in the US, Europe, and the rest of the world in cutting interest rates and how this had steadied worldwide stock markets, jittery in the face of uncertainty and a reduction in confidence.[3]

» An article on consolidation in the food and drink industry cites Budweiser and Heineken as part of "an elite group of global brands recognizable to consumers anywhere."[4]

» US venture capital firm Greylock is reported to be expanding its operations to Europe and Israel, because "All the companies we invest in will, at some point, be global companies."[5]

» In soccer, Chelsea beat Tottenham Hotspur 3-2, with goal scorers including Marcel Desailly (born in Ghana, plays internationally for France) and Jimmy Hasselbaink (born in Surinam, previous clubs include Portugal's Boavista and Spain's Athletico Madrid).[6] Chelsea's squad, the most international in the English Premiership, also includes Danish player Jesper Gronkjaer, Italians Carlo Cudicini and Gianfranco Zola, Swiss Italian Roberto di Matteo, Icelandic Eidur Gudjohnsen, Nigerian Celestine Babayaro, Dutchmen Winston Bogarde, Ed De Goey and Mario Melchiot, Australian Mark Bosnich,

Yugoslavian Slavisa Jokanovic, and Frenchmen William Gallas and Emmanuel Petit.[7]

In many ways the world feels much smaller than ever before – international travel is faster and easier; satellite communications mean that even the remotest parts of the world can be contacted almost instantaneously; Web technologies allow people to work together even if they are physically far apart; the Internet brings information to everyone just about everywhere; and multinational agreements, for example within Europe, mean that living and working in another country is something that is relatively simple to arrange.

As globalization becomes ever more significant, it is more and more important for managers in all businesses to gain some kind of international experience. As a *Harvard Management Update* comments, "If you don't get overseas experience at some stage of your managerial career, you're probably not going to make it to the corner office in the ever more global 21st century."[8]

WHAT THIS BOOK IS ABOUT

This book looks at the personal side of working globally – the benefits and disadvantages of working away from your home country, the problems of culture shock and the skills of working with people of different nationalities. It discusses the opportunities and challenges facing freelance and other independent workers in the global economy and looks at the resources and sources of information on which they can draw. Through stories of expatriates and global travelers it explains what it takes to survive in an international environment and the characteristics of the most effective global executives.

The book also considers the broader developments underlying the growth of a global workplace, such as the information and communications technologies that have made long-distance work a real possibility, in particular the growth of the Internet. It takes a brief look at the wider societal issues raised by globalization and its impact on the less developed economies. Finally, it draws on the advice of management writers and experts in the field to offer guidelines for success.

NOTES

1 McLuhan, Herbert Marshall (1962) *The Gutenberg Galaxy: The Making of Typographic Man*, University of Toronto Press, Toronto.
2 Hill, Andrew (2001) "Giuliani says hope of finding survivors is 'very small'", FT.com, September 18.
3 Wolffe, Richard (2001) "Kohler sees hope for economic recovery among the wreckage", *Financial Times*, September 20.
4 Jones, Adam (2001) "Reaching markets other beers can't", *Financial Times*, September 19.
5 Campbell, Katharine (2001) "Greylock plans to grow in Europe and Israel", *Financial Times*, September 19.
6 Owen, David (2001) "Leeds seize an early advantage", *Financial Times*, September 17; www.chelseafc.co.uk.
7 www.chelseafc.co.uk.
8 Billington, Jim (1996) "Should you take that foreign assignment?", *Harvard Management Update*, August, 8-9.

Definition of Terms

This chapter explores what working globally means.

» Who is working globally?
» Why work globally?
» How many are working globally?

The concept of working globally covers a number of situations, from the relatively straightforward to the much more nuanced. If you are working globally you may be an expatriate working for part of a large organization or a self-employed worker on contract to another organization; or you may be part of a team of people from different nationalities and may be based in different places; or you could just be a frequent flyer who travels on business.

WHO IS WORKING GLOBALLY?

Nancy Mueller, a consultant in cross-cultural communication and the author of *Work Worldwide*, answers the question "Who works abroad?" in this way: "People just like you. Working expatriates are many and varied, including seasoned executives who are hired for the short- or long-term to fill strategic management positions. These may be new jobs, created to establish a base of operations in a particular country, or already established positions. Expatriates also include globetrotters who have made a career of pursuing job opportunities around the world, professionals who reside in [their home country] but do frequent business abroad, employees who are working abroad to develop their knowledge and skills used at home, partners of professionals sent abroad, and adventurers seeking income to finance their travels around the world."[1]

A report from the Centre for Research into the Management of Expatriation (CReME) at Cranfield University, UK, defined four forms of international working.

» *"Expatriate assignment:* defined as an assignment where the employee and family move to the host country for a specified period of time, usually over one year.
» *Short-term assignment:* an assignment with a specified duration, usually less than one year. Family may accompany employee.
» *International commuter:* an employee who commutes from the home country to a place of work in another country, usually on a weekly or bi-weekly basis, while the family remains at home.
» *Frequent flyer:* an employee who undertakes frequent international business trips but does not relocate."[2]

In CReME's survey among multinational companies, 53% had more than 50 employees on expatriate assignments, and the figures were 18% for short-term assignments, 6% for international commuters and 26% for frequent flyers. All forms of working globally were on the increase.[3]

WHY WORK GLOBALLY?

In many organizations and industry sectors, global experience is considered to be a vital part of an executive's development – if all business is global, it has to be run by global managers. Many individuals also find international work and travel beneficial for their personal development and widening their perspectives.

More specifically, the CReME survey found that expatriate assignments were used for skill transfer, managerial control and management development. Short-term assignments were primarily for skill transfer, although occasionally for management development. Skill transfer was again the main reason for international commuting assignments, followed by managerial control, family reasons, and the cost factor. In contrast, managerial control was the prime reason for frequent flyer assignments, followed by skills transfer, developing an international cadre, costs, and family reasons.[4]

Consultancy McKinsey views expatriates as "the cornerstone on which international ventures are built."[5] Since many businesses face a shortage of skilled professionals, a strong pool of global talent is a strategic asset and a source of sustainable competitive advantage. The benefits of expatriates are:

» They transfer know-how and technologies, typically from head office.
» They build country-specific knowledge and relationships.
» They develop the local talent that will lead to longer-term success and profitability.

McKinsey reports that although many companies focus on using international managers with particular technical skills for short-term assignments, the most successful organizations build a team of people who know how to build and expand a foreign business, and then bring in additional technical experts when necessary.

HOW MANY ARE WORKING GLOBALLY?

It is very difficult to establish statistics for the number of people working globally, particularly because of the temporary nature of some of their assignments and because many work on an international basis without leaving their home base.

The Institute for Employment Studies expresses the problem thus: "Labour market researchers who rely on traditional methods find themselves suddenly helpless. It is as though we are entomologists who have been trained to study caterpillars. An armoury of methods has been devised for tracking their exact characteristics, rates of growth and movements . . . But suddenly . . . they become butterflies. No longer obliged to proceed, a footstep at a time, in linear fashion over physical surfaces, they can take off into a third dimension and fly in any direction, landing we know not where. The rules which enabled one to predict their movements no longer apply."[6]

However, some idea of the numbers involved in formal expatriate assignments is given by United Nations statistics, which identify 53,000 companies as multinationals with 450,000 affiliated companies worldwide. The top 100 global companies employ more than six million foreign nationals.[7] Add to that the vast numbers of people either employed by or on contract to smaller companies outside their home country, and those who merely travel on business or who service international customers from a home base, and you are talking tens of millions of people working globally.

And the flow of the global workforce is in all directions. The traditional image of an expatriate is a Westerner taking their expertise to the developing world and benefiting from an exclusive and privileged lifestyle in return. As Hilary Harris of Cranfield puts it: "The word 'expatriate' conjures up images of colonial outposts, gin and tonics at the club and lavish benefits for pioneering men bringing enlightenment to far flung corners of empire."[8]

In fact, to take just one example, of the 26.3 million immigrants in the US (defined as people living there who are foreign born and have permission to stay permanently), the 722,000 foreign workers from India take the highest proportion (20%) of each year's issue of H1B visas, which are for speciality occupations such as high technology. Out of all immigrant groups in the US, Indians have one of the highest per capita incomes. One of the biggest venture capital firms reports that 40% of its portfolio is companies founded or managed by people of Indian origin and there are Indians in high-profile jobs, such as Rono Dutta who is president of United Airlines, or Rajat Gupta, managing director of McKinsey & Co.[9]

Taking advantage of the opportunities for global working leads to a global patchwork of cultures and experiences that is both challenging and fascinating, and that is what we will be exploring in the rest of this book. First, a look at the developments that have brought us to where we are today.

NOTES

1 Mueller, Nancy (2000) *Work Worldwide: International Career Strategies for the Adventurous Job Seeker*, John Muir Publications, Emeryville, CA.

2 CReME (2000) "New forms of international working: trends and HRM implications", Centre for Research into the Management of Expatriation, Cranfield.

3 *Ibid.*

4 *Ibid.*

5 Hsieh, Tsun-Yan, Lavoie, Johanne and Samek, Robert, A.P. (1999) "Are you taking your expatriate talent seriously?", *McKinsey Quarterly*, 3, 70–83.

6 Huws, U., Jagger, N. and O'Regan, S. (1999) *Teleworking and Globalisation: Towards a Methodology for Mapping and Measuring the Emerging Global Division of Labour in the Information Economy*, Institute for Employment Studies, Brighton.

7 Solomon, Charlene Mariner (2000) "The world stops shrinking", *Workforce*, January.

8 Harris, Hilary (1999) "The changing world of the expatriate manager", Centre for Research into the Management of Expatriation, Cranfield.

9 Spaeth, Anthony (2000) "The golden diaspora", *Time*, June 19.

The Evolution of Working Globally

What is the context to today's global village? How long have we been working globally, and what developments have led to our being able to do so more easily than ever before? This chapter takes a look at:

» the development of management and multinationals;
» air travel;
» global communication;
» computer technology.

Traders and merchants have been traveling to other countries to sell and distribute goods since the beginning of written history, certainly since the Greek and Roman empires. Nevertheless, until the fifteenth century Asia and Europe remained relatively self-contained, with trade between the two dominated by Italian cities, particularly Venice. Colonialism began around 1500 when the Europeans discovered a sea route around Africa's southern coast and reached America. The emerging nation states of Portugal, Spain, the Dutch Republic, France, and England spread European institutions, culture, and trade throughout the world.

Although there was some movement of workers from the agricultural areas into the towns from as early as Mesopotamian times, widespread migration of labor to other countries did not begin until the start of the sixteenth century, when the Spanish government licensed the importation of African slaves to work in its colonies.[1] As well as slaves there were also obviously settlers from Europe. For example, as well as the Dutch, the settlers in New Amsterdam (later to be renamed New York) included French, Scandinavian, Irish, German, and Jewish inhabitants.[2]

The development of the modern multinational can also be traced back as far as joint-stock companies such as the East India Company, established by the English in 1600, and its rival, the Dutch East India Company. These companies were very powerful, with a monopoly of navigational rights and the ability to make treaties with native princes, establish garrisoned forts, and appoint governors and justices.[3]

Trade and emigration continued, with the largest migration in history being that from Europe to North America beginning in the 1840s. Between 1880 and 1910 some 17 million Europeans reached the US, for example.[4] Most of this kind of migration was, however, for economic or political reasons, not necessarily as a matter of choice. It was not until the twentieth century, when the growth of management as an occupation combined with the explosion in service industries and greater availability of both international transport and communication, that working globally became both a real possibility and an aspiration.

THE GROWTH OF AIR TRAVEL

Commercial air travel began in Florida, US in 1914, with a flight across 22 miles of Tampa Bay between Tampa and St Petersburg. Developments were interrupted by the First World War, but recommenced in 1919 when the first airline was founded, the Deutsche Luftreederie, which began service from Berlin to Leipzig and Weimar.

In the 1920s the only long-distance routes were those connecting countries such as Britain and France with their colonies where landing rights could be negotiated along the way – the maximum distance that could be flown without stopping to refuel was then 500 miles, ruling out crossing the Pacific or the Atlantic. But by the early 1930s Pan American, the British Imperial Airways and the Dutch KLM were trying to develop world-scale routes, using the new kind of seaplane.

Larger fuel loads needed to travel long distances required more powerful engines, achieved by using four-engined planes, and the first transoceanic passenger flight took place in 1936.

Transatlantic routes continued to be flown during the Second World War, and there was rapid growth in air traffic in the decade after 1945. By 1957 there were more passengers crossing the Atlantic by air than by sea, and jet planes came into service during that year.[5] Air travel has continued to become more extensive and faster ever since and international air transport is the fastest-growing sector of the transportation industry.[6]

The number of people now boarding aircraft every day would have been unimaginable to the pioneers of air travel. The number of scheduled air passenger journeys has grown from around 9 million in 1945 to some 1.5 billion in 1999.[7] The ten busiest airports in 2000 were in Atlanta, Chicago, Los Angeles, London, Dallas, Tokyo, Frankfurt, Paris, San Francisco, and Amsterdam.[8] Before the terrorist attacks in the US in September 2001, which may well lead to a reduction in the number of journeys undertaken, air traffic was predicted to rise by an average annual rate of 4.5% in the first decade of the twenty-first century, and well above average in the Asia-Pacific region.[9]

Over half of passenger journeys are now travel for leisure rather than business,[10] partly driven by a reduction in the cost of air travel in general and partly by people's desire to travel more widely. Although there are still a significant number of people traveling on business trips every day, more and more business people are trying to find ways of reducing their travel requirements. Achieving this aim has been facilitated by improvements in communications technology.

GLOBAL COMMUNICATION

The most pervasive means of communicating with someone in another country is of course by telephone, patented by Alexander Graham Bell in 1876 and now available almost everywhere in the world thanks to satellite and mobile communications technology.

The first commercial communications satellite was Intelsat I, launched in 1965, and communications satellites now transmit telephone, television and data services between various points worldwide. There are also several large networks planned of non-geostationary satellites in low-Earth orbit, which will provide a service for wireless telephones, faxes, pagers and car radio terminals, and will offer truly global coverage, including the far north and south that can't be reached by the current geostationary satellites.[11]

Although a primitive form of mobile telephony was introduced in the US as early as 1946, the first cellular system in use was in Japan in 1979. A number of other systems were developed in Europe, but they were incompatible with each other. In 1988 a group of telephone companies within the European Community began operating the digital global system for mobile (GSM) communications, the first to allow a user of a mobile phone in one European country to "roam," using the same phone in another subscribing country.[12] In addition to phones, personal digital assistants and laptop computers are able to use the mobile network to connect to the Internet, and this is technology that is continuing to develop.

Methods of sending written rather than verbal communication instantaneously to another person began with the telex. The international telegraphic message-transfer service consists of a network of teleprinters and each subscriber has an assigned call number. The message is typed on the teleprinter keyboard, converted to an electrical signal and transmitted over channels leased from the telephone system to be printed or stored at the destination teleprinter. Telex systems originated in Europe in 1930 and are still in use where high transmission speeds are not necessary or in areas where more modern equipment is not available.[13]

Telex was superseded by facsimile transmission (fax). The fax machine scans printed material and transmits the information through the telephone network to another machine, where it is reproduced in a form close to the original. Fax transmission can also take place between computers via fax software and a modem. The first commercial (telegraph-based) facsimile system was introduced in 1863 between Lyon and Paris by Italian inventor Giovanni Caselli, but it was not until 1974 that a worldwide fax standard was issued, known as Group 1. These machines could transmit one page in about six minutes.

Fax machines remained too cumbersome and expensive until the introduction of the Group 3 standard in 1980, which used digital transmission and could send one page in under a minute. Since then the price of fax machines has declined and their use by businesses and in private homes has grown. There are now tens of millions of fax machines across the world, although the use of fax has declined significantly since the development of electronic mail.[14]

COMPUTER COMMUNICATION

The development of computing technology and then the Internet has also greatly facilitated the exchange of information and opinions worldwide. Computers originate in various technologies, but the first automatic digital computer (ruled so by a judge in 1973) was the Atanasoff-Berry Computer, the prototype for which was designed in 1939. The first real-time computer, the Whirlwind, became operational at Massachusetts Institute of Technology in 1951, designed by Jay Forrester, the originator of the field of system dynamics, and Ken Olsen, who co-founded Digital Equipment Corporation. Development was increasingly rapid thereafter, including the following highlights.

» The first IBM stored-program computer was the 701, initially shipped in 1953.
» This was followed by second-generation transistorized computers, the 1620 and the 1790, in 1959.
» The first minicomputer, the PDP-1, was developed at Digital in 1960, the same year that removable disks appeared.
» By 1961 IBM computers were able to communicate over the telephone line using a modem.

» The third-generation IBM was the System 360, an integrated circuit-based computer, introduced in 1965.
» IBM's first minicomputer, the System/3, began shipping in 1969.
» The System 370, the fourth-generation IBM, was introduced in 1970.
» Intel's first microprocessor, the Intel 4004, was developed in 1971, the same year that engineer John Blankenbaker built the first personal computer, the Kenbak I.
» In 1975 Microsoft was founded by Bill Gates and Paul Allen and the first computer store opened.
» Two years later in 1977 Apple Computer was founded and introduced the Apple II personal computer with a graphical user interface.
» By 1980 the total number of computers in use in the US exceeded one million.
» In 1981 IBM entered the personal computer market.
» In 1982 *Time* named the computer its "man of the year."[15]

The origins of the Internet lie in a US Department of Defense network called ARPANET (Advanced Research Projects Agency Network), commenced in 1969. The National Science Foundation took over the TCP/IP (Transmission Control Protocol/Internet Protocol) technology that was the basis for the communications protocol and established in 1983 a distributed network of networks, what we now know as the Internet.[16]

The first main uses of the Internet were for electronic mail (e-mail), file transfer, remote computer access via telnet, bulletin boards and newsgroups. Then in 1989 Tim Berners-Lee invented the World Wide Web, providing a graphical interface to make navigation of Internet sites much easier. Via a Web browser such as Mosaic or its successor Netscape Navigator, users were then able to "point and click" with their mouse rather than entering reams of computer code to move around Websites or from one site to another.[17]

An indication of the extraordinary power of the Internet is given by this description from a group of computer scientists involved in its development: "The Internet is at once a world-wide broadcasting capability, a mechanism for information dissemination, and a medium for collaboration and interaction between individuals and their computers without regard for geographic location."[18] The Internet itself has now become almost a "commodity," a global information infrastructure supporting other commercial services such as Internet telephone or audio and video streaming.

The ways in which the Internet and Web technologies are being used to facilitate working globally are discussed in Chapter 4. The box below is a timeline summarizing the evolution of global communications.

TIMELINE OF THE EVOLUTION OF GLOBAL COMMUNICATIONS

» **1500**: Beginnings of colonialism
» **1600**: Establishment of East India Company
» **1840**: Start of mass migration from Europe to North America
» **1863**: First commercial facsimile system introduced
» **1876**: Telephone invented
» **1914**: Commercial air travel commences
» **1919**: First commercial airline founded
» **1930**: First telex system established
» **1936**: First transoceanic passenger flight
» **1951**: First real-time computer
» **1953**: First IBM stored-program computer
» **1957**: First jet plane in service
» **1959**: Introduction of second-generation transistorized computers
» **1960**: First minicomputer
» **1961**: IBM computers communicate via modem
» **1965**: Introduction of third-generation IBM; first commercial communications satellite launched
» **1969**: Establishment of ARPANET; introduction of first IBM minicomputer
» **1970**: Introduction of fourth-generation IBM
» **1971**: First microprocessor and first personal computer
» **1972**: First e-mail sent
» **1974**: Group 1 fax standard introduced
» **1975**: Microsoft founded and first computer store opened
» **1977**: Apple Computer founded and Apple II introduced
» **1979**: First cellular phone system
» **1980**: Number of computers in US exceeds one million

» **1981**: First IBM personal computer
» **1982**: Computer named *Time*'s "man of the year"
» **1983**: National Science Foundation establishes the Internet
» **1988**: GSM established
» **1989**: World Wide Web invented

NOTES

1 "Work, history of the organization of", *Encyclopædia Britannica*, www.britannica.com/eb/article?eu=115711&tocid=67043.

2 "Colonialism", *Encyclopædia Britannica*, www.britannica.com /eb/article?eu=108616&tocid=0&query=colonialism.

3 *Ibid.*

4 "Human migration", *Encyclopædia Britannica*, www.britannica. com/eb/article?eu=42394&tocid=0&query=human%20migration.

5 "Transportation, history of", *Encyclopædia Britannica*, www. britannica.com/eb/article?eu=120011&tocid=0&query=history %20of%20transportation.

6 Button, Kenneth (1999) "The usefulness of current international air transport statistics", *Journal of Transportation and Statistics*, May, 71-92.

7 Jeanniot, Pierre J. (2000) "The future of the airline industry", speech by Director General and CEO of IATA to the *Economist Global Airlines Conference*, London, May 16.

8 Airports Council International (2001) "World airports ranking by total passengers - 2000 (Preliminary)" Airports Council International, Geneva, March 26.

9 Xinhua News Agency (2001) "UN agency predicts steady growth in air traffic in coming decade", Xinhua News Agency, June 14.

10 Jeanniot, Pierre J. (2000) "The future of the airline industry", speech by Director General and CEO of IATA to the *Economist Global Airlines Conference*, London, May 16.

11 "Satellite communication", *Encyclopædia Britannica*, www. britannica.com/eb/article?eu=67541&tocid=0&query=satellite %20communication.

12 "Telephone and telephone system", *Encyclopædia Britannica*, www.britannica.com/eb/article?eu=119002& tocid=76210&query=radio%20telephone.

13 "Telex", *Encyclopædia Britannica*, www.britannica.com/eb/ article?eu=73460&tocid=0&query=telex.

14 "Telephone and telephone system", *Encyclopædia Britannica*, www.britannica.com/eb/article?eu=119002&tocid=76236.

15 Information on the development of the computer drawn from "A chronology of computer history", www.cyberstreet.com/hcs/ museum/chron.htm and "Chronological table", www.fht-esslingen. de/telehistory/chrtable.html.

16 "Internet", *Encyclopædia Britannica*, www.britannica.com/eb/ article?eu=1460&tocid=0&query=history%20of%20the%20- internet.

17 "World Wide Web", *Encyclopædia Britannica*, www.britannica. com/eb/article?idxref=40278.

18 Leiner, Barry M., Cerf, Vinton F., Clark, David D., Kahn, Robert E., Kleinrock, Leonard, Lynch, David C. *et al.* (2000) "A brief history of the Internet", Internet Society (ISOC), www.isoc.org/internet/ history/brief.html.

The E-Dimension

How has the Internet affected and facilitated global working? This chapter explores:

» communication developments, such as e-mail, Internet telephony, Web conferencing, team collaboration tools;
» job hunting via the Internet – recruitment Websites and freelance marketplaces.

Despite only having been made widely available through the invention of the World Wide Web in 1989, the Internet is now a global phenomenon. The latest results from the Internet Software Consortium's twice-yearly survey indicate that there are 109 million connected computers (hosts) in 230 countries and territories. The Internet is expanding at the rate of 63 new hosts and 11 new domains per minute worldwide.[1]

Although the largest number of connections are, as would be expected, in countries such as the US, Japan, and the UK, large increases were experienced in the first half of 2001 in several African countries, and many others such as Panama (417%), Vietnam (220%), and Bangladesh (200%).[2]

In addition to the obvious benefits of the Internet for activities such as shopping, travel reservations, and banking, there are some other uses that are particularly welcome to those working globally.

COMMUNICATION

E-mail can be a boon in areas where the postal service is unreliable and long-distance phone calls are expensive. "E-mail changed the lives of expatriates wherever there was a reliable telephone service," says Joanna Parfitt, editor of *Women Abroad*. "I remember how I looked forward to the soothing messages and empathy of friends when, once repatriated, I felt so strangely alone in my own country. And how I, in turn, would do the same when they moved on themselves."[3]

One step on from e-mail is instant messaging, where you can see if the person you want to talk to is online and exchange typed messages with them instantaneously, but at the cost of your Internet connection rather than an international phone call. The service is offered by various companies, including AOL (www.aol.com/aim/download.html), Microsoft (http://messenger.msn.com), ICQ (www.icq.com) and Yahoo! (http://pager.yahoo.com/). Some of the services offer voice connections or will do so in the future. The downside is that these various products are not compatible with each other, so you may need to have a number of different instant messaging programs if you want to communicate with a lot of people in this way.

The cost of international telephone calls can be considerably reduced by using voice-over IP, or Internet telephony. It allows you to use your

PC (or, for some services, your Mac), as long as it is equipped with a sound card and a microphone, to make telephone calls to a normal phone almost anywhere in the world at vastly cheaper rates. There are details of some of the main Internet telephony providers in the resources section, Chapter 9.

For dispersed teams, innovations such as electronic conferencing mean closer collaboration and fewer feelings of isolation. They also reduce the need to travel to a physical meeting, thus cutting costs. Using conferencing services such as those provided by WebEx (www.webex.com), participants can hold audio- and video-linked meetings via their Web browser, including viewing the same documents and manipulating words or objects on the screen. This could be used by, for example, designers who want to suggest changes to an advertisement layout. Virtual meetings via WebEx are free for up to four participants with a one-hour time limit. Web conferencing systems are also offered by companies such as Avaya (www.avaya.com) and PlaceWare (www.placeware.com).

Companies such as Cogos Consulting (www.cogos.com) can set up virtual team spaces on the Internet where participants can manage projects collaboratively, exchange e-mails, and access their own libraries of documents and online communities. This is particularly useful in organizations where sharing knowledge is vital, such as research and development departments or consultancies. Companies offering similar digital workplaces include eRoom (www.eroom.net) and MagicalDesk (www.magicaldesk.com).

Peer-to-peer (P2P) file sharing made headlines in the music world recently with the controversy over Napster, but the technology also has applications in the business world. Groove Networks, Inc. and its founder Ray Ozzie are at the forefront of these developments. The company's aim is to get "the right people together with the right information, the right tools, at the right time – to get things done."[4] Its technology lets groups share files, have instant message conversations or mark up a virtual whiteboard, whatever program or platform they are using on their own computer.[5]

Groove has built-in security and all data is encrypted when being transferred. The benefits of this kind of technology are that it provides in one place on the desktop "a comprehensive, easy to use resource for voice conversations, file sharing, web browsing, joint document creation, threaded discussion, scheduling, decision histories and ad hoc problem solving – all the assets that are otherwise found in a somewhat random series of e-mails, telephone and conference calls, fax transmissions and overnight package deliveries."[6] This can be invaluable for helping a worldwide team collaborate more effectively.

Other companies providing group collaboration and web meeting capabilities include Ezenia! (www.ezenia.com) and IBM with Quick-Place (www.lotus.com/products/qplace.nsf/homepage/$first).

BEST PRACTICE: AO INTERNATIONAL

AO International is a software company supplying database-oriented workgroup publishing solutions to clients such as newspapers, magazines and advertising agencies. It offers three systems: Campaign (content management for catalogs, merchandise, retail, and advertising clients, to manage campaigns), Sam/AdmaN (archiving solution and advertising bookings, sales, production), and Phoenix (newspapers and magazines). These are available for multiple operating systems and database drivers. The company has development agreements with Quark XPress and Adobe and is partnering with other companies, including both IBM and Apple, as a solutions provider.

AO's customers are currently in Belgium, Canada, France, Germany, Indonesia, Thailand, the UK, and the US. Its administrative office is in Brussels, Belgium, but it has a network of offices and home offices in Brussels, London, Glasgow, Bournemouth and Reading in the UK, four locations in Germany, and others in Israel, New Zealand, and the US.

Mike Dolan, one of the company's three managing directors, comments that they wouldn't want to work any other way, because the network of developers they use wouldn't want to be physically located in the same geographic area. However, it does mean that there is none of the informal day-to-day contact that there would be in a normal office.

"We like to have meetings, we like to get together, we like to exchange ideas," Dolan says. "As we've spread out more physically we've tried to find technology to help bring us together and bring a degree of 'real' office life. We've tried to make it as much of an interactive process as possible.''

The company uses group scheduling and team coordination software called TeamAgenda that allows everyone to see each other's calendar. It also has ''always on'' ADSL (Asymmetric Digital Subscriber Line) and cable connections and Webcams using iVisit software. This allows multi-party video, voice and text chat over the Internet, so that AO's staff can talk to and, if they choose, see each other whenever they like.

There is an FTP (File Transfer Protocol) server in Brussels to which everyone in the company has access, which operates on two levels. People working for the company can download important files, prices and so on; users and customers can gain access via a user name and password, to download software updates and obtain answers to frequently asked questions. In addition there is a public-access Website, currently hosted in the US but which may be relocated in the future.

Because the customer base is widely spread, there is no way the company could set up offices in each country where it has a customer. Even if it had engineers in that particular city, they could not necessarily get to the customer's offices in time to resolve a problem. Therefore AO has access to its customers' systems so that its engineers can diagnose faults and provide solutions online. This is much quicker than needing to visit each site.

When people are working independently loneliness and isolation can be a problem, for example not feeling close to your colleagues. Dolan explains: ''You start to imagine all sorts of things that are not true and there's nobody there to bounce the ideas off, to prevent things getting out of hand. The more isolated somebody is, the more wild the fantasies become.''

E-mails and phone calls can help, but chatting via something like iVisit is more powerful. ''You know when somebody comes into the office, for example, because you'll suddenly get a message or they'll speak to you through the computer just to say hi and have a brief conversation about what they're doing. You're not actually face to face but if they have a webcam you can see them so it feels more friendly. It restores the human dimension."[7]

FINDING A JOB

Internet technology is facilitating two shifts in the recruitment industry generally: from the expensive headhunter to the far more economical online recruitment company, and from the company to the job seeker, who has far more knowledge of what positions are available across a wide spectrum of sources. This is significant in the global market for jobs, where being able to access details on the Web provides even greater mobility.

Forrester Research forecasts that the revenues of Internet recruiters will increase from just over $1bn in 2000 to $7bn by 2005.[8] The same research found that two-thirds of UK job seekers with access to the Internet used recruitment Websites, particularly if they were middle managers. It is not only in Europe and the US that people look for a job this way – there are more than 200 employment Websites in China.[9]

Advertising on recruitment sites on the Internet is much cheaper than advertising in traditional media, so more and more companies are using online recruitment. And is it much easier for those looking for a job – no longer do they have to spend days visiting agency after agency, they can find out extensive information from the comfort of their desk and they can arrange to be e-mailed by certain Websites when relevant new positions are advertised. It is also now far easier to get a "snapshot" of the job market in a particular country or sector from, for example, a searchable jobs database.[10] Post your resumé on a number of jobs databases and the employers may well come to you rather than the other way around.

Once you have decided to apply for a certain job, the Internet can also help you find out a great deal of information about that company and its markets. You can visit its own Website, but also search sites such as FindArticles.com or FT.com for the latest press coverage. An Internet search will give you links to forums and Websites about the company, both positive and negative. For example, a Google.com search on Intel provides links to FACEIntel (Former And Current Employees of

Intel) and IntelZone, which offers press information and hosts forums; a search on Nike gives links to sites providing information about the company's labor practices, such as Boycott Nike and NikeWatch.

Other services are or will become available to make the process of finding a job much easier, particularly for those working globally. Some sites offer online psychometric testing, for example, and there are links to numerous tests at www.namss.org.uk/jobassess.htm. Visit www.discusonline.com and you can find out your own behavioral profile. Fitability Systems (www.fitability.com) offer companies an online interview and service for pre-screening, which is in fact a form of assessment test that the candidate completes in about 15 minutes.

Teachers4Alaska.com offers the facility for candidates to post audio and video clips of their answers to common interview questions, recorded with a standard tape recorder or video camera and then converted by the site to QuickTime format. As videoconferencing becomes more generally available and cheaper, companies will be able to conduct interviews by video link. SearchLINC is a commercial Internet video network that provides video capability to desktop PCs and to booths in some hotels, so that recruiters can conduct interviews online and also participate in virtual job fairs.[11]

For those who work on a freelance basis, the Web offers many opportunities for selling their services globally. Sites such as the Free-lance Work Exchange (www.freelanceworkexchange.com) connect freelance professionals with companies who are looking for their services, in fields such as graphic design, information technology, writing and editing, research, consulting, translation, marketing and sales. You can exhibit your resumé and bid for projects that employers post on the site, as well as in some cases seeing competing bids, which can be helpful for deciding whether your price is in line with the marketplace. In many cases the work is completed over the Internet and so your geographic location is largely irrelevant.

There are details of a selection of recruitment and freelance Websites in the resources section, Chapter 9.

NOTES

1 Rutkowski, Tony (2001) "Internet survey reached 109 million internet host level", www.ngi.org/trends/TrendsPR0102.txt.

2 *Ibid.*

3 Parfitt, Joanna (2001) "It's a wired world", *Woman Abroad*, 6, 1.

4 www.groove.net/

5 Kharif, Olga and Salkever, Alex (2001) "A chat with the master of P2P", *Business Week*, August 1.

6 www.groove.net/products/overview/business.

7 Source: author's interview with Mike Dolan; www.ao-international.com.

8 Quoted in Featherstone, James (2001) *"Better net working"*, http://expat.ft.com.

9 BBC Monitoring Service (2001) "China: Rapid growth of online job recruitment", BBC Monitoring Service, February 2.

10 StepStone (2001) "Job hunting on the web", www.stepstone.com/artikler/makethewebwork.html.

11 www.virtualjobfair.com/HRdept/searchlinc.html.

The Global Dimension

This chapter discusses issues such as:

» What is the current attitude to globalization in society at large?
» Is it a good or a bad phenomenon?
» How can companies respond to the challenges of globalization?
» Is the free movement of labor always beneficial?
» How can multinationals move towards sustainable development?

It may seem strange in a book on working globally to have a chapter on the global dimension, but there is a broader issue underlying the tendency for people and companies to seek to work and operate abroad, and that is something that has recently been receiving rather a bad press: globalization.

Globalization is defined by the International Monetary Fund as "the international integration of goods, technology, labor, and capital."[1] In a wider definition, the *Encyclopaedia Britannica* explains it as "the process by which the experience of everyday life, marked by the diffusion of commodities and ideas, is becoming standardized around the world."[2] This is referring to what is known as the "McDonaldization" of society, and the pervasive effect of Western, usually American, culture, particularly movies and television.

A report from the International Monetary Fund in 1997 addressed the question of whether increased globalization should lead to concern. The authors concluded: "There is a common belief that globalization harms the interests of workers, especially unskilled workers, either directly through immigration or indirectly through trade and capital mobility ... these beliefs appear to be at odds with the empirical evidence that globalization has only a modest effect on wages, employment, and income inequality in the advanced economies ... Moreover, the belief that globalization threatens wages and jobs is contradicted by the historical evidence that free trade and the mobility of labor and capital improve global welfare and tend to improve national welfare for all countries involved."[3]

However, globalization had become a dirty word by the time it reached the front pages with a vengeance during street protests and riots against global capitalism at high-profile meetings including the World Trade Organization in Seattle, US in 1999, the World Bank and International Monetary Fund in Washington DC, the World Economic Forum at Davos, Switzerland in 2000, and the G-8 summit in Genoa, Italy in 2001.

It is not only the anti-capitalism protesters, often called anarchists in the press, who have strong words to say about the effects of unchecked globalization. At the 2001 World Economic Forum – termed the "annual celebration of globalization" by the *International Herald Tribune*[4] – representatives of developing countries were invited to put their side of the argument. Their criticism was scathing, "saying that everything from inequities in trade rules and import barriers in industrialized countries to a shortage of aid and capital flows was denying developing countries many of the potential benefits of globalization."[5]

However, as *Time* comments, globalization is not an optional extra, it is a fact of life: "The problem with globalization is that it will not go away because we don't like some of its worrisome implications or its destabilizing impact. The process is irreversible, if only because of the information technology and communications revolutions."[6]

There are some significant issues that are going to have to be addressed in relation to the economic, social, and ecological consequences of big business worldwide. *The Guardian* gives some examples: "How are the ecological limits of a finite planet to be respected in the face of policies designed to promote never ending growth? How is the widening gap between rich and poor to be closed when many of the signals that companies respond to are designed to reward greed? How can the needs of the 10bn people who may inhabit this world in 2050 be met without drastic changes to consumption patterns?"[7]

Business Week catches the new mood: "In the late 20th century, global capitalism was pushed by leaps in technology, the failure of socialism, and East Asia's seemingly miraculous success. Now, it's time to get realistic. The plain truth is that market liberalization by itself does not lift all boats, and in some cases, it has caused severe damage to poor nations. What's more, there's no point denying that multinationals have contributed to labor, environmental, and human-rights abuses as they pursue profit around the globe."[8]

So how are companies responding? Oil companies are in a sector that receives a great deal of criticism for its ecological impact. The case study below shows how Shell has addressed some of the challenges.

BEST PRACTICE: ROYAL DUTCH/SHELL

Shell is one of the multinationals most singled out as a villain by anti-globalization protesters. It was criticized for its role in the Nigerian oil industry's damage to the environment in Ogoniland, particularly when Ogoni activist Ken Saro Wiwa was hanged by the Nigerian government. It also sparked backlashes in 1995 when it tried to dump the Brent Spar oil platform at sea and was forced to back down.[9]

In 1996 Shell announced its commitment to "make sustainable development part of the Shell culture."[10] It produced a new internal code of conduct, its "General Business Principles," to which it expects all employees, contractors and suppliers to adhere. The principles cover its responsibilities to its stakeholders and society, and with regard to economic considerations, business integrity, political activities, health, safety and the environment, the community, competition, and communication.

Breaches of the principles are not tolerated. For example, Mark Moody-Stuart, former chairman of the Committee of Managing Directors, comments: "We enforce zero tolerance of bribery, political payments and unfair trade and competition." As a result, in 2000 106 contracts were terminated and two joint ventures divested because of incompatibility with the principles, and four incidents of bribery resulted in seven dismissals of staff.

In Shell's view sustainable development is a holistic endeavor, which must pay equal attention to all aspects of the company's operations and impact. Mark Moody-Stuart explains: "The truly sustainable development of a society depends on three inseparable factors: the three-legged stool. The first leg is the generation of economic wealth, which companies deliver better than anyone else. The second is environmental improvement, where both government and the company have to play their role. The third leg is social equity. Companies have a role to play here, but the main responsibility rests with civil society as a whole, including government."

Shell publishes a report every year on its progress and performance, which can be surprisingly candid in relaying other people's criticisms. For example, in the 2000 report, "People, planet and profits," as well as complimentary remarks from various sources the company includes statements from Shell employees such as:

- "Staff in Shell are mere numbers to management not people for whom Shell has any sense of care or responsibility."

> » "We're still emitting too much CO_2 into the atmosphere. What this company needs is a good Greenpeace scare and we'll find the money."
> » "Shell always put emphasis on HSE but do NOT think about their employee's long working hours. It's a lack of commitment and inhuman."
>
> The report also includes information on initiatives the company is taking to put right some of the problems it has caused. For example, it is sponsoring community development in the Niger Delta to the tune of tens of millions of pounds, with an emphasis on community participation. The programs include health, education and agriculture, concentrating on initiatives that promote long-term development and empower communities.
>
> One beneficiary is the Adagwe Grammar School, Nigeria, whose head teacher explains: "We had been crippled by a shortage of science teachers and the total lack of a laboratory. But that started to change when Shell posted some science teachers . . . and came to our aid by building and equipping a laboratory. This has given our pupils a much better chance of becoming our scientists of the future."[11]

TALENT WARS

One of the consequences of globalization is labor mobility. A shortage of skilled professionals in Western economies means that it is easy for the most talented people from developing countries to find jobs abroad. Western Europe is forecast to face a shortage of 1.7 million IT professionals by 2003 and this is not merely a high-tech problem: 50,000 construction jobs remain unfilled in France and there are insufficient accountants and chemical and metallurgical engineers in Europe generally.[12]

However, this "brain drain" can lead to difficulties in the developing economies that people are leaving. A paper in 2001 from consultancy McKinsey reported the possibility that it "will have lasting economic repercussions on the developing world, robbing it not only of the skills of these workers but also of their influence on the productivity of others."[13]

As an example of the size of the problem, about 33% of R&D professionals in developing economies have left those countries to work in the US, the EU or Japan.[14] The main reason for leaving is that there is a lack of comparable career opportunities at home, something that up to now developing nations have done little about.

Migrant workers may experience personal problems that their managers either are not aware of or don't care about. Liam Campbell, who has been involved in construction projects with people of up to 14 different nationalities including some from North Africa, explained:

> "Most people coming here experience huge problems securing accommodation, bank facilities, police problems with registration etc. Generally speaking the people in charge have no comprehension how the guy is feeling. He is in a strange environment with very little time to contact his family. His wages may not be paid on time because he has not had the time off from work to open a bank account. His wife has the phone number of his hotel and is calling for money to feed the children, and he is expected during all of this pressure to be civil to people in the office."[15]

Expatriates from developing countries do remit significant amounts of money to their families back home and thereby contribute to the local economy; the World Bank estimates that annual remittances from economic migrants are some $67bn.[16] Nevertheless, Kevin Watkins, senior policy adviser at international aid agency Oxfam, comments: "What developing countries need is skilled people to stay in them. Developing countries make enormous sacrifices to educate people up to university level and rich countries then reap the dividend."[17]

There are beginning to be better opportunities in developing countries, however, particularly in new technology. "Developing countries are accelerating the migration [from places such as Silicon Valley]," reports the *Industry Standard*, "sweetening the rewards for high-tech workers by pushing development in their technology sectors, cutting taxes and loosening immigration laws."[18] This is a trend that bodies such as the International Labor Organization (ILO) and the United Nations are keen to encourage.

THE GLOBAL COMPACT

In 1999 United Nations Secretary-General Kofi Annan proposed the Global Compact, challenging business leaders to help build the social and environmental pillars needed to make globalization work. He explained that the Western economies took globalization for granted, but that "it is a much tougher sell out there, in a world where half of our fellow human beings struggle to survive on less than two dollars a day."[19]

The Global Compact incorporates nine principles covering human rights, labor, and the environment, drawn from the Universal Declaration of Human Rights, the ILO's Fundamental Principles on Rights at Work and the Rio Principles on Environment and Development. It asks participating companies to act on these principles in their own corporate domains.[20]

Several hundred companies have signed up to the Global Compact, including ABB, BASF, Bayer, BP Amoco, BT, Crédit Suisse, First Boston, DaimlerChrysler, Deloitte Touche Tohmatsu, Ericsson, Nike, Novartis, Pearson, Rio Tinto, Royal Dutch/Shell, SAP, Statoil, Unilever and Volvo. They are expected to integrate the principles into their business practices, become public advocates for the initiative, and at least once a year to report via the Global Compact Website (www.unglobalcompact.org) on concrete steps they have taken.[21]

The UN is particularly keen for companies and organizations from developing countries to participate in the Global Compact so that its impact is truly worldwide and in the spirit of real sustainable development. For instance, 30 Indian companies are active participants; there have been meetings of business leaders of eight African countries to discuss the main issues; and executives in Thailand have formed a task force to promote the principles and develop a strategic plan for their implementation.[22]

NOTES

1 Slaughter, Matthew J. and Swagel, Phillip (1997) "Does globalization lower wages and export jobs?", International Monetary Fund, Washington DC.

2 Watson, James L. (2001) "Globalization", *Encyclopaedia Britannica*, www.britannica.com/original.

3 Slaughter, Matthew J. and Swagel, Phillip (1997) "Does globalization lower wages and export jobs?", International Monetary Fund, Washington DC.

4 Buerkle, Tom and Friedman, Alan (2001) "Globalization foes have their say: poor countries unleash a barrage of criticism at Davos Forum", *International Herald Tribune*, January 27.

5 *Ibid.*

6 Smadja, Claude, (1999) "Living dangerously", *Time*, February 22.

7 Juniper, Tony and Wainwright, Hilary (2001) "Worlds apart", *Guardian*, January 31.

8 Engardio, Pete (2000) "Global capitalism: can it be made to work better?", *Business Week*, November 6.

9 Chalmer, Patrick (2001) "Firms stumped for anti-globalisation response", Reuters, September 24.

10 van der Veer, Jeroen (2001) "Principles in practice", Group Managing Director of Royal Dutch/Shell Group, speech at Caux Round Table, London, September 10.

11 Source: www.shell.com; "People, planet and profits," Royal Dutch/Shell Group, 2000; Jeroen van der Veer, Group Managing Director of Royal Dutch/Shell Group, "Principles in practice," speech at Caux Round Table, London, September 10, 2001; Precious Omuku (2000) "Community development in Nigeria," www.shell.com/royal-en/content/0,5028,29273-52218,00.html.

12 Graff, James (2000) "Help wanted for Europe", *Time*, June 19.

13 Devan, Janamitra and Tewari, Parth S. (2001) "Brains abroad", *McKinsey Quarterly*, 4.

14 Brown, Mercy and Meyer, Jean-Baptiste (1999) "Scientific diasporas: a new approach to the brain drain", prepared for the *World Conference on Science*, Budapest: United Nations Educational, Scientific, and Cultural Organization.

15 E-mail correspondence with author.

16 UNESCO Sources (1998) "A mobile, borderless world", *UNESCO Sources*, January.
17 Turner, David (2001) "Developing countries 'must use expatriate talent'", FT.com, August 20.
18 Pappas, Leslie (2000) "Brain gain", *Industry Standard*, August 7.
19 "UN launches new effort on Global Business Compact", World Economic Forum press release, January 28, 2001.
20 "The global compact: what it is – and isn't", United Nations, www.unglobal-compact.org/un/gc/unweb.nsf/webprintview/whatitis.htm.
21 "Global Compact Newsletter", July 27, 2001, www.unglobal-compact.org/un/gc/unweb.nsf/webprintview/newsletter.htm.
22 *Ibid.*

The State of the Art

This chapter takes a look at current research into and experience of working globally, considering the areas of:

» global leadership;
» preparation for working globally;
» culture shock;
» living abroad;
» women working globally;
» trailing partners;
» potential dangers of working globally;
» repatriation.

GLOBAL LEADERS

A three-year study by Hal Gregersen, Allen Morrison and J. Stewart Black, funded by Brigham Young University and detailed in their book *Global Explorers*,[1] found that 85% of Fortune 500 firms surveyed did not think they had enough global leaders. "Most companies lack an adequate number of globally competent executives," they report. "We found that almost all companies claim that they need more global leaders, and most want future global leaders of higher caliber and quality."[2]

If the record number of foreign-born CEOs running major companies in the US, the UK and many other countries is anything to go by, that situation may be beginning to change.[3] For example:

» Christine Lagarde, chairman of US commercial law firm Baker & Mackenzie, is French.
» Sidney Taurel, chairman, president and CEO of US healthcare company Eli Lilly & Co., is Moroccan.
» Jacques Nasser, president and CEO of US automotive company Ford Motor, is Lebanese and grew up in Australia.
» Bo Lerenius, CEO of Associated British Ports plc, is Swedish.
» Paolo Scaroni, group CEO of British glass company Pilkington plc, is Italian.

Furthermore, an article in *Chief Executive* reports:

"The international executive community has produced striking examples of executives who have honed their business skills in countries outside their own and then achieved great success in their home countries. In addition, the past few years have seen a series of international deals involving mega-mergers, joint ventures, and strategic alliances ... If [this] trend continues, there will be an increasing demand ... for a steady flow of internationally experienced executives."[4]

What training and orientation do individuals require to prepare them for an international career? And what are the obstacles they are likely to encounter on their travels?

PREPARATION FOR WORKING GLOBALLY

As business becomes more global and more people work on an international basis, an increasing number of companies and individuals are investing in cross-cultural training. A *Harvard Management Update* puts this succinctly: "Why is the world an oyster for some businesspeople but a barnacle for others? Simple: successful managers prepare themselves before conducting business around the globe. They learn how to adapt to unfamiliar business cultures."[5]

Language training is significant because, as consultancy McKinsey comments, "Anyone who relies solely on English as the worldwide business language will be unable to tap into valuable local sources of business information and influential business networks and can have only a limited ability to conduct negotiations."[6]

Cross-cultural training is valuable for people at all levels of an organization who are likely to be working in multinational teams or negotiating with customers or suppliers from other countries. It is also obviously vital for someone who is about to embark on a posting overseas, and for their family if they are going as well. What should the preparation consist of?

» As a minimum, and only a minimum, information about other countries' history, politics, economy, and culture.
» Training in cross-cultural sensitivity, including role plays and psychological evaluations.
» Building and managing a multicultural team.
» Negotiation from different cultural perspectives.
» Exploration of other values and belief systems.
» Cultural stereotypes.
» Perceptions of hierarchy and authority.
» Dos and don'ts in behavior and etiquette.

"The concrete things are easy – the laws, the policies protocol, how to exchange a business card, how to conduct yourself in public, social distance," according to Professor Robert Bontempo of Columbia Business School. "The hardest thing to do is get a psychological understanding of the extent to which your own culture brings with it a set of biases that limit your effectiveness."[7]

Gregersen et al.'s research, quoted above,[8] claims that there are four strategies for developing effective global leaders.

» *Travel* – this is real travel, not the normal, cocooned kind of executive travel. So get off the beaten track and find out what local life is really like.
» *Teams* – work with people with different background and perspectives.
» *Training* – on topics including international strategy, change management, cross-cultural communication, international business ethics, multicultural team leadership, managing in uncertainty.
» *Transfers* – overseas assignments, living and working in a foreign country. Some 80% of executives in this study identified this as the single most influential experience of their lives.

CULTURE SHOCK

Culture shock (see definition in Chapter 8) can be experienced by anyone going to work in another country or culture for any length of time. At the beginning you will probably be excited and exhilarated by the newness of everything, but after a while most people get depressed and homesick to some degree.

"Some [managers] are able to adapt in an almost chameleon-like way to different countries whereas others cling desperately to their habits and national approaches," comments Elisabeth Marx, author of *Breaking through Culture Shock*. "Some international executives are highly successful while others struggle with basic everyday activities. We now know that it is our ability to manage culture shock in international business that makes a difference between failure and success."[9]

Rolando Soliz, director general of Vance International, a security services company in Mexico, explains some of the difficulties:

"Surprisingly, the most common complications facing newly transplanted expatriates concern basic necessities easily taken for granted at home. Examples include local law enforcement customs, emergency response services, and means of public transportation. Learning how these and other basic services function can present significant challenges to new residents . . . While getting a flat tire fixed or selecting a new school may be relatively painless at home, learning to do either in another country may not be so simple."[10]

You do not have to be living in a totally different culture to your own to experience culture shock. For example, someone moving from one European culture to another may not think they are going to have much of a problem and not do too much preparation, but in fact it is the very similarity that leads to the most disorientation when things fail to operate in the way you expect. Speaking the same language may also not be a guarantee of familiarity, as those traveling between the UK and the US can readily attest.

So what does culture shock feel like? It may be described as homesickness, but it is more than a vague sense of the blues. You may experience difficulty with the most ordinary activities: because the shops are different you may not be able to buy what you need easily; or you may have problems communicating, even if you know something of the language, because you don't understand people's everyday expressions. Your automatic routines, the things you used to do all the time without thinking about them, are no longer valid and this can lead to frustration and anger. You may become like a recluse and shut yourself away because making new friends seems too much of an effort, or you may be moody and cry for no apparent reason.

How do you deal with culture shock? The following suggestions may help.

» Give yourself sufficient time to settle in. Accept that things will be different, but try to see it as part of the fun of living somewhere new. Don't expect too much of yourself.
» Familiarize yourself with your new surroundings and find out as much as possible about how everyday activities operate. Realize that you can't change the rules; instead, work out how to live within them.
» Try to develop a new routine to replace your old one as soon as possible.

» Talk to other people about how you feel – they may have been through the same problems and can help convince you it is entirely normal.

» Join an expatriate network or social club to help you make new friends.

» Read the local newspapers and find out what is going on.

» If you don't speak the local language, learn as much as you can, or find someone to translate for you, at least initially.

» Use e-mail to keep in touch with friends and family back home. Bringing small familiar objectives or your favorite food from home can help.

» Don't make "them and us" comparisons – accept that varied ways of life are equally valid and celebrate the differences.

EXPATRIATE LIFE

In order to assess whether a foreign assignment is right for you, a *Harvard Management Update* recommends that you ask and answer the following questions:[11]

» Does your company truly value foreign experience? Have senior managers worked extensively abroad? Does the company invest in making sure that international postings are a success?

» Does your industry truly value foreign experience? If it tends to favor technical specialization over a general management education, a foreign assignment may not be the best move.

» How much do you want to work abroad? "Choosing a country or language because it is trendy suggests a lack of the necessary conviction. Sticking power born of a personal passion for the posting is what matters."[12]

» Can your family handle it? Involve them in the decision from the start.

Expatriate postings are not always successful. Failure rates for overseas jobs can be as high as 70% in developing countries,[13] with typically between 15 and 25% of other assignments ending prematurely, particularly those involving US expatriates.[14] There can also be a problem of the best expatriate managers being "poached" by other organizations.

There are costs in failure for both the individual and the organization. An unsuccessful expatriate can find that their career is severely damaged and can experience a loss of confidence and self-esteem. The financial cost to the company is estimated by consultancy McKinsey to be as high as $1mn per posting, including time and money invested in selection, visits to the location, training, and relocation.[15] Careful selection in the first place is obviously therefore a priority, as is suitable training and other preparation for both expatriates and their families.

A survey of 160 multinational expatriates by the London School of Economics and expatriate Website Homezick.com investigated the challenges faced by expatriates and their families. The key findings were as follows.[16]

» 60% said that the main reason for leaving their home country was career opportunity.
» Family/marital reasons were the main cause of moving abroad for nearly 25% of women but only 10% of men.
» Just over 50% said that their employer had not lived up to their expectations in providing support before the move and on arrival. Assistance with finding accommodation was the main need.
» 49% reported that the quality of life in their host country was better. There were home country differences in this: improvement was experienced by 66% of British expatriates, 43% of Norwegians, 42% of Swedes and only 29% of Americans.
» The most important information to have was news from their home country for 90% of respondents.
» 93% of respondents had access to the Internet and 62% had access at home and at work. The Internet was used for information, communication, and news, as well as by 57% for shopping.

WHERE ARE THE WOMEN?

Research in the US reports that although women hold 49% of middle management positions, only 13% of expatriates working for US corporations are women.[17] Another study by PricewaterhouseCoopers among companies in Europe found that only 9% of expatriate managers were women,[18] and other sources put the figure at between 10 and 15% of all assignments.[19] Why is this the case?

Catalyst, a New York-based advisory organization for women in business, surveyed 1,000 current and former expatriates and their spouses and also frequent flyers, global managers who merely travel abroad rather than relocating. Catalyst claims that women are being held back by others' preconceptions about their willingness to travel and their ability to relate to people from other nationalities. Its findings were as follows.[20]

» Survey respondents believe that women are not considered as "internationally mobile" as men, although women frequent flyers in the study were more likely than the men to say that they would relocate in the future.
» The assumption is that women are less effective than men at conducting business with foreign nationals, but only 23% of women expatriates reported having had difficulty building host-country relationships.
» Women are assumed to have more constraints on their work/life balance than men, while in the survey roughly half of both men and women say that they find striking a balance difficult.
» Being selected in the first place is the greatest hurdle for women.
» Women on international assignments are often more isolated than their male counterparts and excluded from the networks and mentor support available to the men.
» Only 55% of women expatriates are married, compared to 78% of men. This suggests that women with family commitments are less willing or able than men to make the sacrifices involved in accepting a foreign assignment.
» Most women expatriates surveyed said that being a woman did not interfere with their ability to do their job; 75% said that being a woman had a positive or neutral impact on doing business overseas.[21]

Since most people of either gender find out about foreign assignments from their immediate boss and since many managers appear to assume that women would not be interested in working globally, women have to *ask* to be considered for an international job rather than being appointed automatically.[22]

Women can have difficulties in another culture because there are varying degrees of cultural prejudice against them in different areas, for example in the Middle East, or where there are fewer women in business such as parts of Asia or Latin America. In some cultures they may not be acknowledged during meetings or their decisions may be questioned. They may be forced to dress differently and not go out alone or in the company of men other than their husbands (if they have one). However, according to Linda K. Stroh, professor of human resources and industrial relations at Loyola University in Chicago, "Even in the more harsh cultures, once they recognized the woman could do the job, once her competence has been demonstrated, it became less of a problem."[23]

In today's working environment where the importance of the softer side of business and of emotional intelligence is being more widely recognized, woman may also be more successful than men in some circumstances. Nina Segal, a career counsellor in international work issues, explains:

"Women's traditionally strong intuitive and interpersonal skills make them a natural choice for work in different cultures, where it is important to read subtle cues and different business styles. It is a win–win situation, for the corporation, for the individual, and for relationships between cultures."[24]

Bill Sheridan, senior director of the New York-based National Foreign Trade Council, has an interesting perspective on the acceptability of women expatriates:

"Western women are accepted, in the most traditional cultures, generally. They are just considered a little different. Some research in the 1980s even suggested that such Western women are considered like a third gender – different from domestic women and obviously not men."[25]

Raj Tatta, a partner with PricewaterhouseCoopers in the US, warns of the dangers of overlooking women's potential contribution:

"This is the tightest labor market the world has ever seen. If you do not draw upon your women for your international assignments, you are hurting yourself. [It] is no longer a matter of good corporate citizenship ... it's a matter of the corporation's survival."[26]

TRAILING PARTNERS

The Catalyst study reported above found that married women are much more likely to have working spouses (91%) than married male expatriates (50%), therefore the availability of spousal support programs is more significant for them.[27] However, many corporate arrangements assume that the spouse is female. BP Amoco's internal publication for trailing spouses is called *Woman*, for example.

Psychologist Leonie Elphinstone conducted research among men of seven different nationalities living as partners of expatriates in ten international locations. She found that most of the men went abroad to help their partner progress their career into an executive-level position. Most expected to work full-time, but because full-time, career-oriented jobs were difficult to locate most worked part-time or studied while abroad. Younger men found this particularly difficult.[28]

The men in the study who took primary responsibility for their young children while abroad welcomed the change to spend more time with their children and develop closer relationships. This change in role was difficult for some: "Learning to accept that your status in life and identity is no longer defined by your job is quite a challenge," comments Elphinstone. "Many of the problems men encounter are not dissimilar to those experienced by the women. What makes the difference is that men are brought up to be bread-winners and when things go wrong they find they have further to fall."[29]

There are so many "trailing male spouses" in Brussels, Belgium, where many international companies are headquartered as well as the European Union and NATO, that a support group has been set up for them, STUDS (Spouses Trailing Under Duress Successfully). Members come from many countries although few are from Asia; possibly Asian men will not accept the role of an accompanying spouse.[30] The network organizes monthly lunches, newsletters and an annual dinner dance, as well as day trips, golf tournaments, children's play groups, and brewery tours. There are currently more than 70 members.[31]

According to the PricewaterhouseCoopers survey in Europe, the number of participating companies whose definition of an expatriate's partner includes "live-in" or same-sex partners has nearly doubled since 1997, to 42%.[32] The definition of dependants has also broadened to include not only stepchildren or children of live-in partners, but in some cases dependent parents.[33]

This is a reflection of the diversity of family situations in society generally, and is something that needs to be taken into account when organizations are deciding on policies for handling the needs of expatriate families. That domestic concerns is a factor is highlighted by two findings from the PricewaterhouseCoopers survey: the main reasons for refusing an assignment were domestic reasons (76%) and the dual career issue (59%); and the main reasons for failure included the intercultural adaptability of the partner, children's educational needs, and the partner's career.

FACING THE DANGERS

One perhaps unexpected side-effect of the increase in working globally is a rise in the chances of an expatriate's being kidnapped while abroad. Colombia, Chechnya, Georgia, Tajikistan, Kyrgyzstan, the Philippines, Yemen, Nigeria, and Angola are the kidnap hotspots.[34] Most are what are termed "economic kidnappings," although oil companies in particular have become vulnerable to protests from local people demanding that a greater share of their wealth remain in the area.[35]

The US Insurance Information Institute claims that kidnappings of foreign nationals increased by 100% to 1,728 between 1985 and 1999,[36] and this may be a conservative figure since the reported cases are estimated to be only 10% of the total.[37] Some 92% of kidnaps end in the victim's release, sometimes for a large sum of money, although governments tend to discourage the payment of ransoms because it encourages the kidnappers to try again. Nevertheless, a report from the London-based think tank the Foreign Policy Centre[38] put the level of ransom payouts at a staggering average of $500mn a year.

As examples, British civil engineer Tim Selby was kidnapped in Bangladesh in February 2001 and freed four weeks later after a shootout between the kidnappers and government commandos. In contrast,

Scottish oil worker Alistair Taylor, held captive by Marxist rebels in the Colombian jungle for almost two years, was only released after payment of some $1mn in ransom by his employer, Texas-based Weatherford.[39]

One reason often cited for global executives being targets is that they may be inexperienced at the dangers of life in regions such as Latin America and Africa. An insurance broker specializing in kidnap insurance commented, "Even some big companies have not given the slightest bit of thought to dealing with security situations abroad. They're sending people abroad who shouldn't be leaving their own village, let along their own country."[40]

The issue of employee safety generally has been much more on companies' minds after the recent terrorist attacks in New York and Washington. Some companies even in traditionally volatile areas appear to have only superficial guidelines. "We have been getting a lot of calls from Pakistan and the Middle East," reports Kerry Parr, an aviation consultant specializing in emergency repatriation for corporate clients, "where there are still organizations which should know better but have done nothing."[41]

Women are often considered to be at greater risk than men, but this is not necessarily the case. "Women take more precautions," says Patti Bellinger, vice president of global diversity and inclusion for BP Amoco. "Men don't feel as at risk [but] there are basic rules of the game when traveling that men and women have to follow."[42]

Information and advice on the security status of particular countries can be obtained from both the US State Department (www.travel.state.gov) and the UK Foreign Office (www.fco.gov.uk).

COMING "HOME"

It is not only before an assignment that training and acculturation must be considered but also at the end, before and after the expatriate returns home. A survey of repatriating US managers by the US Bureau of National Affairs[43] found the following:

» 68% of managers were unsure what their next positions would be when they returned;
» 77% saw their return as a demotion;

» 91% felt their companies didn't appreciate their international experience;
» 69% suffer from "reverse culture shock";
» 25% of repatriated managers move to another organization within a year of returning, taking with them their knowledge and expertise.

In another survey,[44] it was reported that 85% of global managers felt that their international experience made them more marketable, but only 60% of current expatriates and 45% of former expatriates believed that their global experience would lead to advancement with their current employer.

Many organizations do little to help repatriate employees. Michael McCallum, US national director of business development for Berlitz International, comments: "Many HR people think all it consists of is moving household goods and making travel arrangements."[45] The International Assignee Research Project, by Berlitz International and the Institute for International Human Resources, found that 77% of expatriates coming home received no career counseling from their employers and only 6% were offered re-entry training.[46]

What preparation can be made for coming home? If you are working for an organization with a head office, keeping in touch with people there can help to ensure that it is not a case of "out of sight, out of mind." Maintaining links with friends and colleagues in the home country is easier with e-mail and the Internet. And financial planning to ensure that you can afford to set up a new household will remove some of the stress, particularly in times of rising house prices.

You will also want to make sure that you keep up to date with news and events in your home country. It is surprising how much can change in a couple of years, politically, socially and professionally. And when you choose the international assignment in the first place, make it one that you can be fairly sure will be valuable in relation to your next career move.

When returning home after working overseas for a while, be prepared for the fact that your overseas assignment will have changed you as well. Libby Royster, an IT consultant in San Francisco who spent two years in Madrid, comments: "You can go home, again, but you'll always leave a part of you behind."[47] You may not want to lose the new identity you took on when abroad: "Going to a new country where virtually no one knows you is terribly liberating. You can reinvent yourself into whoever you wish to be. Going home sometimes means facing yourself and your past."[48]

Chris Westphal, author of *A Family Year Abroad: How to Live Outside the Borders*, agrees:

> "Don't expect coming home to be easy: in many ways, it was harder to return home than it was to leave. Unconsciously, we expected everything to be the way it was when we left, and that wasn't the case ... The best route to adjusting to life back home is to get involved, and bring to new undertakings the resourcefulness, perspective, and energy that you will have developed while living overseas."[49]

NOTES

1 Gregersen, Hal, Morrison, Allen and Black, J. Stewart (1999) *Global Explorers: The Next Generation of Leaders*, Routledge, London.
2 *Ibid*.
3 Lyons, Denis B.K. (2000) "International CEOs on the rise", *Chief Executive*, February.
4 *Ibid*.
5 Harvard Management Update (1999) "Prepare for that overseas business trip!", *Harvard Management Update*, April, 8-9.
6 Hsieh, Tsun-Yan, Lavoie, Johanne and Samek, Robert A.P. (1999) "Are you taking your expatriate talent seriously?", *McKinsey Quarterly*, 3, 70-83.
7 FT.com (2000) "The world-wise employee", FT.com, March 6.
8 Gregersen, Hal, Morrison, Allen and Black, J. Stewart (1998) "Developing leaders for the global frontier", *Sloan Management Review*, Fall.
9 Marx, Elisabeth (2000) "Culture shock unwrapped", *Woman Abroad*, www.womanabroad.com.
10 Workforce (2000) "Getting smart about going global", *Workforce*, July.

11 Billington, Jim (1996) "Should you take that foreign assignment?", *Harvard Management Update*, August, 8–9.

12 *Ibid.*

13 Hsieh, Tsun-Yan, Lavoie, Johanne and Samek, Robert A.P. (1999) "Are you taking your expatriate talent seriously?", *McKinsey Quarterly*, 3, 70–83.

14 Bross, J. and Matte, S. (1997) *Selecting International Employees: A Corporate Investment*, Family Guidance International, Toronto.

15 Hsieh, Tsun-Yan, Lavoie, Johanne and Samek, Robert, A.P. ((1999)) "Are you taking your expatriate talent seriously?", *McKinsey Quarterly*, 3, 70–83.

16 Reported in Fasken, Hugh (2001) "Uncovering the real world of the expat", FT.com, March 8.

17 Windham International/National Foreign Trade Council/Institute for International Human Resources (1999) *Global Relocation Trends*, Windham International, New York.

18 PricewaterhouseCoopers (2000) "International Assignments European Policy and Practice: Key Trends 1999/2000", PricewaterhouseCoopers, London.

19 van der Boon, Mary (2001) "Brave new world", *Woman Abroad*, www.womanabroad.com.

20 Catalyst (2000) *Passport to Opportunity: US Women in Global Business*, Catalyst, New York.

21 Townsend, Kerry (2001) "The best place for women", FT.com, January 16.

22 Tyler, Kathryn (2001) "Don't fence her in", *HR Magazine*, March.

23 *Ibid.*

24 Segal, Nina (2001) "We want you! Why women aren't going global and why they should", *Work Abroad*, www.international.monster.com/workabroad/articles/women/.

25 Townsend, Kerry (2001) "The best place for women", FT.com, January 16.

26 Tyler, Kathryn (2001) "Don't fence her in", *HR Magazine*, March.

27 Townsend, Kerry (2001) "The best place for women", FT.com, January 16.

28 Elphinstone, Leonie (2001) "When the males trail", *Woman Abroad*, www.womanabroad.com.

29 *Ibid*.

30 Dieter, Miu Oikawa (2000) "Brussels rich in 'househusbands' of expatriate wives", Kyodo World News Service, May 31.

31 www.expataccess.com/social/studs/studs.htm.

32 PricewaterhouseCoopers (2000) "International Assignments European Policy and Practice: Key Trends 1999/2000", PricewaterhouseCoopers, London.

33 *Ibid*.

34 Overell, Steven (2001) "Kidnap: the global executive's nightmare", *Financial Times*, May 25.

35 Chiahemen, John (2001) "41 Mobil workers seized on Nigerian island", Reuters, June 27.

36 Reported in Overell, Steven (2001) "Kidnap: the global executive's nightmare", *Financial Times*, May 25.

37 Gooder, James (2001) "There must be some way out of here ... and that's the chequebook. Economic kidnapping is on the rise and big business is desperate for a solution", *Independent on Sunday*, July 15.

38 Reported in Odell, Mark (2001) "Colombia, Mexico, Brazil hot spots for kidnapping", *Financial Post – Canada*, April 23.

39 Gooder, James (2001) "There must be some way out of here ... and that's the chequebook. Economic kidnapping is on the rise and big business is desperate for a solution", *Independent on Sunday*, July 15.

40 Odell, Mark (2001) "Colombia, Mexico, Brazil hot spots for kidnapping", *Financial Post – Canada*, April 23.

41 Cohen, Amon (2001) "How to stay safe amid dangerous liaisons", FT.com, September 24.

42 Tyler, Kathryn (2001) "Don't fence her in", *HR Magazine*, March.

43 Quoted in Hsieh, Tsun-Yan, Lavoie, Johanne and Samek, Robert, A.P. (1999) "Are you taking your expatriate talent seriously?", *McKinsey Quarterly*, 3, 70–83.

44 Catalyst (2000) *Passport to Opportunity: US Women in Global Business*, Catalyst, New York.

45 Poe, Andrea, C. (2000) "Welcome back", *HR Magazine*, March.

46 Quoted in Poe, Andrea, C. (2000) "Welcome back", *HR Magazine*, March.

47 Royster, Libby (2001) "Even cowgirls get the blues", *Escape from America Magazine*, 5.
48 *Ibid*.
49 Westphal, Chris (2001) "Top tips for expats", *Escape from America Magazine*, 5.

In Practice

Case studies of people working globally in various environments:

- » a management consultant living in Germany;
- » an IT project manager working in the Netherlands;
- » an executive search consultant in London;
- » an academic and entrepreneur in the US;
- » a writer in London.

The case studies in this chapter have been deliberately chosen to reflect a range of experiences different to that of the traditional expatriate. These are not tales of managers sent abroad by their companies and buoyed up by corporate support systems. Instead, they are stories of people who are working globally in a new way, networking and collaborating with varied groups and organizations all over the world, and finding new blends of home and abroad.

ROWAN GIBSON: GLOBAL NETWORKING

Rowan Gibson, author of the international bestseller *Rethinking the Future*,[1] is a management consultant, writer, and speaker. Born and educated in the UK, he lives with his German wife and two young sons near Düsseldorf, Germany.

Gibson is founder and chairman of Rethinking Group, a network organization with team members in Germany, the Netherlands, and Belgium. The company offers a mix of business intelligence and marketing creativity, developing what it calls "core strategies" for a number of international clients.

"I've spent pretty much my whole career working exclusively for international companies," says Gibson. "We've never accepted clients who were purely interested in their own home market. That's not our thing. We've built a specialism out of creating core strategies that work for our clients internationally. Many of them have their headquarters in Holland, Austria, Germany, Belgium, the UK, and the US, but all of them have been looking for an international or even global approach."

Rethinking Group's network organization brings together a number of independent consultants in various countries (Gibson's partner Peter Barrett-Jones, for example, is an Englishman who is based in Belgium). The group has its own design team in the Netherlands, made up entirely of freelance professionals.

All business is global

"All business is global today at some level," says Gibson. "As soon as you're dealing with a company's top management and the bigger challenges they face, you find that sooner or later you're looking at global issues. And that means that you need to start working with a collection of people who are based in different parts of the world. The great advantage now is that we can network electronically with these people in a way that makes geography increasingly irrelevant.''

One example is a global project that Rethinking Group coordinated for US-based office furniture giant Steelcase. The project was called Revolutions @ Work and resulted in an international trade show, a documentary film, a 112-page book, a corporate advertising campaign and other activities. It involved people from the UK, mainland Europe, the US, Canada, and Australia, many of whom never physically met each other, and was completed within only a few months thanks to the team's network-based way of working.

Gibson explains: "Networking tends to delinearize work. Everybody can be working on the same project simultaneously in a nonlinear fashion, communicating via phone calls and e-mails that cross geographic borders and time zones. It gets jobs done in three months instead of three years. I can't imagine how we could possibly achieve what we do, in the time we do it, without this decentralized, network approach."

One of the discoveries Gibson has made is that network organizations waste less time and energy on navel gazing, office politics and gossip than traditional hierarchical organizations. "We're in constant contact with each other via phone and e-mail. But we find that we're only talking about client-related or project-related issues. When we meet, it's to talk about the project, not about ourselves."

But how do you control a network organization? "We don't," replies Gibson. "You only need hierarchical control in an organization where people need to be told what to do. But when you've got a team of top professionals together, there's an intuitive understanding about what to do that emerges from the group. In biology they call it 'emergent control,' like you find in a flock of birds or a swarm of bees. We provide leadership in the sense that we set the direction for the strategy, but the team members play their own respective roles and use their own specialisms to bring that strategy to life. We don't have to motivate anybody or tell them what to do. They make up their own minds about what is right, even if they are making decisions at 12 o'clock at night."

Home and away

Gibson himself travels a great deal: "If you ask my wife if there are any disadvantages of working globally she'd say, 'I don't like it when Rowan has to travel, because it isn't down to the local high street, it's usually to some other country. Not only is he away for longer, but travel is getting riskier.' That is a fact of life in modern business. There are so many people I know who are in the same situation: tomorrow they'll be in Vienna, the day after Munich, the next week in Washington. You can't say 'I'm sorry I can't come' because the meeting happens to be in another country or on the other side of the world. Our clients are global and they expect us to be global too."

In a typical week – and he comments wryly that there's no such thing – Gibson is normally working at home three days and away for two, either traveling or at one of the Rethinking Group offices. If he is away for a week or more, as is sometimes necessary if he has to travel to the US or the Far East, he tries to arrange things so that he can take a week off afterwards with the family.

His work routine is a deliberate strategy to allow him to spend more time with his children: "One of the great advantages if you are able to work at home is seeing more of the family. The boys are only going to be 7 and 5 once in their lives. I think we're learning from the mistakes of the last generation, who never saw their kids growing up because they were too busy working."

He runs his working life with the help of new technology: a cell-phone, a laptop, the Internet, a fax and a palmtop. "You can now work globally from where you are. It doesn't necessarily mean getting on planes and flying around the world. The cellphone and the Internet have changed all that. I literally run global projects from my home office. You could never have done that a few years ago."

Nevertheless, working at home does create the temptation never to stop working. "The nature of global project work is that you can't plan ahead in a linear way. Projects don't wait in a queue, they come at you from all sides and all at once. You've always got at least 25 things on your to-do list. But I have to admit that my home office is probably my favorite part of the house, so it has a sort of magnetic effect on me."

Particularly because of time zone differences, Gibson's working hours need to be flexible, but that can have two sides to it: "In the summer I often choose to stop working after lunch, go outside for some sunshine with the kids, and do the work in the cooler evening hours. It's a much more balanced and civilized way of life and, at the same time, I'd argue that it's a much more productive one."[2]

KEY LESSONS

» If you're doing global work you need to involve global people.
» Working globally demands flexibility.
» Networked global teams can achieve more in less time.

MIKE GARBE: AWAY FROM THE FAMILY

Mike Garbe is a British freelance IT consultant, currently managing the building of two operational systems acceptance environments at the European Patent Office in The Hague, the Netherlands. He has 27 years' experience in the IT industry in the UK. Prior to moving to the Netherlands, he was experiencing difficulties in finding a new project to work on and he also wanted to have some foreign work experience on his CV.

Garbe has found it a beneficial experience working with people of many different nationalities. His team consists of two British, one Australian, and a Frenchman. The director is French and in the department there are British, French, Belgians, Dutch, Swedes, Germans, Italians, and Russians. All other EU nations are represented in the organization.

The management style is very different to that prevailing in the UK. "Having people working for me that are used to the UK style of management and work ethic is a big plus. The main problem we as a group have is in implementing change within the department. This takes a long time, far longer than in the UK."

One of the main personal problems that Garbe has faced is that his Thai wife and their young children have stayed at home in the UK and not moved with him. "They are not terribly happy at my being away, but it was not uncommon for me to have to live away in the UK as well," he explains. "It is the nature of consultancy work."

"I manage to get home almost every weekend. In fact, there is often less traveling involved in getting from my home in the UK to my apartment in the Netherlands, which takes three and a half hours, than there was previously in getting to work in London, where there were frequent train delays and cancellations!''

Nevertheless, Garbe says that on his next assignment he will definitely take his family with him, particularly since he is thinking of trying to find work in Asia.

Finding your feet

Garbe came over to The Hague the day before he started work, so that he could settle in and find his way around. He recommends that anyone should allow themselves at least this time so that they don't plunge straight into work and feel disorientated.

The hotel his agent found was a 45-minute tram journey away from work, but he was able to find a more local hotel for the second week and a well-situated apartment three weeks later. "I got the local hotel with help from people at work and the apartment had just been bought by a member of staff as an investment. I think the trick is to get something temporarily and then put out feelers at work to find a more permanent solution," he suggests.

In relation to life in the Netherlands he has the following comments, which give an indication of the issues that expatriates need to face:

» Finding your way around on the tram system in The Hague and Amsterdam is easier if you buy a street plan (light blue cover) that shows tram and bus routes. They are available at most stations and airports and are town specific.
» Most shops shut at 17.30, except on Thursday which is late night shopping in The Hague. "The supermarket by my apartment is open till 22.00 during the week, much to the amazement of even the Dutch." Shops in The Hague Centrum, Schreveningen (a beach resort by The Hague) and Amsterdam have started opening on Sundays. All other shops are shut then, so you need to plan ahead. Also on Mondays most shops don't open until midday.
» "There is a lot more jostling on the street than even in London. And when it's busy you need sharp elbows to get on a tram, train or bus!"
» The Dutch don't mind keeping you waiting to be served while they talk.

» The PIN debit card system is very good. "You swipe the card and type in your PIN on the keypad and that's it. No signing and they are accepted almost everywhere."

» "Expect to wait a long time at a bank or a travel agent's, but they don't hurry you when it's your turn."

» Dutch bars operate differently. You only pay when you leave and are expected to leave a tip. "Also don't expect a full beer glass - if it's over half full you are doing OK. This is accepted here and if you complain they will put it right, but with very bad grace."[3]

KEY LESSONS

» You may need to learn a different style of management.
» It can be difficult if you can't take your family with you.
» Even the basic things in life may be very different in another country.

ELISABETH MARX: COPING WITH CULTURE SHOCK

Elisabeth Marx is a director of Norman Broadbent, an executive search firm in London. Born and educated in Germany, she moved to the UK to do a PhD and post-doctoral studies at Oxford University. She then held a lectureship at the National University of Singapore before returning to the UK eight years ago to work as a psychologist at Norman Broadbent. There she also conducted research on management issues and subsequently moved into international executive search. She is the author of *Breaking through Culture Shock*.[4]

In her current role Marx searches worldwide - from Hong Kong to Washington - for executives who can help companies to internationalize. She also considers the management structure of those companies from a strategic perspective and advises them of new roles they may need in order to compete globally. Other work is on the development of the top team and integrating teams in different locations, such as London and New York.

Culture shock

Marx came straight to Oxford after her master's degree and didn't have much time for preparation. The language problems she experienced initially disappeared fast, but she found it more taxing understanding the subtleties of English language and behavior, which are far more indirect than the German. She also found a need to develop her social skills to encompass small talk and the more flippant English style at drinks parties, rather than the more formal and serious German approach.

When she moved from the UK to Singapore, Marx underestimated the differences that she would find in what was superficially a very modern, high-tech and international city state. The university was run according to the British model and she appeared to settle in very quickly: "The culture shock crept in much later when I realized I didn't understand a single thing that was going on."

What she grew to understand was that everyone's behavior was determined by their individual background, even if they appeared very Western and had been educated internationally. For example, in departmental meetings, the expatriates would argue and debate vigorously; the Singaporeans would stay calm, try not to offend anyone and attempt to bring the discussion together. Marx learnt a great deal from this about influencing indirectly, rather than in an assertive Western way.

She also found it unusual to have to deal with the Chinese's natural respect for authority, particularly of teachers and lecturers. What she taught was accepted as absolutely true, and it was difficult to get her students to challenge her. In contrast, one of the main legacies of her time in Singapore was realizing the necessity of turning her own assumptions on their head and asking herself what she could learn from the way other people deal with life and business issues.

In general she found Singaporeans quite inspiring, because of their entrepreneurial spirit, pragmatic approach to business and great motivation.

Strategies for survival

Marx comments that whenever you go to a new country, the first couple of weeks make you unbelievably tired, particularly if you are having to speak another language. In Singapore it was especially difficult because of the heat, she felt lethargic and was unable to sleep properly.

Her way of handling this is to leave one box of her belongings packed and to have a mental escape route: "If it gets tough I say to myself I can go back, I can drop it all, I don't have to stay here if I can't stand it." She has never left a location early, but says the psychological boost of knowing she would be able to has helped her to cope.

She has been in the UK for eight years and has a great attachment to London, which she sees as home. She goes on to explain, "My home is where I am, right now, or wherever I go next." As someone who has traveled extensively, ideally she would like to have several homes.

She recommends the following strategies for those working globally:

» Have a good idea of what you are letting yourself in for by collecting as much information as possible about the country and its people.
» Know yourself very well and be aware how much of a challenge the move is going to be. Know how far you can push yourself before you decide things are not working.
» Understand the physical and psychological demands on you and reduce stress wherever possible. It helps if you are someone who can deal with uncertainty.
» Seek out sources of social support as a buffer against culture shock, either among expatriates or locals. This helps you feel a sense of belonging and to retain perspective.
» If you find yourself reacting in surprising ways, ask others in a similar situation whether this is normal; if not, seek help before matters get out of hand.

The global experience

Marx finds working in foreign environments very exciting because you are constantly on your toes and learning all the time: "You can't get complacent, you just have to adapt." She comments that international experience helps you become much more flexible and come up with more creative solutions.

An international job can be very demanding and stressful, however, and not everyone is suited to it. She sees a problem with expecting executives to have international experience if they are not temperamentally suited to it, because forcing someone to work abroad is not a recipe for success. Living in too many locations can make you somewhat rootless and have a negative effect because you become too detached and lack continuity in your life.

Working globally is important for career development but in her view more significant for an individual's personal development: "It improves and broadens your social skills and means that you approach every situation with a sense of curiosity. You learn not to make too many assumptions and to look at things with a fresh eye."[5]

KEY LESSONS

» Keep an open mind and question your automatic assumptions.
» Know how far you can safely push yourself.
» Find your own psychological escape route.

MICHAEL LISSACK: LEARNING FROM FAILURE

A former investment banker with Smith Barney who used to travel some 300,000 miles a year, Michael Lissack gained renown in the US after blowing the whistle on the illegal and unethical practices of some Wall Street firms.

Since 1995 he has been an academic, teaching economics at Williams College, Massachusetts, US; research techniques at Henley Management College and complexity at the London School of Economics in the UK; business strategy at IMD in Lausanne, Switzerland; and business ethics at the Rotterdam School of Management, the Netherlands, Vanderbilt University, Tennessee, US, and Keele University, UK.

Lissack is also one of the founders of the Institute for the Study of Coherence and Emergence. This virtual community has 40 academic fellows from around the world who work together on research projects, publications and speaking engagements and who meet at a conference twice a year. It has a journal, *Emergence*, of which Lissack is editor-in-chief, whose production team has members based in the Netherlands, the UK and the US.

He is also an entrepreneur, having founded several Internet start-up companies in the US and Europe, and has been an angel investor in several more. However, he has now sold all of these apart from Knowledge Ventures Inc., an Internet technology company that assists the academic sector with online research. This company is in the process of developing a tool to check citations and monitor plagiarism.

Managing at a distance

Lissack comments that he has learnt a great deal from the failure of some of his ventures, perhaps more than from the successes. He has sound advice for entrepreneurs trying to run companies at a distance.

One company that he founded in the Netherlands, for example, was developing a software platform for integrating content and knowledge technologies within companies. The Magi technology allowed a user with one click of a mouse to locate other people in their company who knew about any highlighted text, or to locate company documents on the same subject. At proof-of-concept stage the product looked excellent, but the developers in the Netherlands were unable to deliver the necessary code to make it work properly (although one of Lissack's other companies did produce a successful version in the US based on the same concept). Not only that, but they were lying about their progress to the on-site manager, who was then unknowingly giving false reports to Lissack.

This was only discovered when the supposedly working product was delivered to a third party for testing before being sold to a client. The third party phoned Lissack to say that there were problems, for example that screens were showing reports that an action had been performed, but it had not in fact been carried out. It was subsequently also found that one of the team had been embezzling from the company.

"It's an old saw, but if something sounds too good to be true, it probably is," comments Lissack. "Telephone calls are no substitute at all for face-to-face communication. On the phone you miss the emotional signals, the body language, that would tell you something was wrong."

His recommendation is that if you don't know the people who are working for you very well, you must either go and visit them yourself on a frequent basis or employ someone who does. Once a month (as Lissack did) is just not enough when dealing with relative strangers. Until you know their emotions and body language you need face-to-face contact. This is particularly the case if they are on another continent and from another culture, where you may miss some obvious red flags.

Secondly, take time out, say a couple of hours once a week, to think about the situation and survey it with a jaundiced eye. This will help you to avoid being carried away with apparent success. If you can't be sufficiently cynical yourself, again, employ an adviser who can.

Thirdly, if you find yourself throwing money at a problem, pull out. Lissack wishes he had done so immediately when the company's expenses began to double, from $200,000 to $400,000 a month. This should have been a danger signal, but he didn't pick it up sufficiently quickly. The on-site managers excused expenses with "It's what we need to get the product finished and on time." (What they meant was, "We don't know what is wrong but if we spend enough surely we'll fix it.") The company has now been sold, but at a significant financial loss to Lissack.

Frequent flyer

As someone who has traveled extensively, Lissack offers the following tips for surviving as a frequent flyer:

» If flying from the US to Europe, take a day flight, don't try to sleep on the plane. This will help avoid jetlag.
» On a long flight if you have to travel overnight, spend the extra money for a bed.
» Check how full the flight is – if the load is light, buy two discounted economy seats rather than traveling business or first class. It will still be cheaper and you will have more space, particularly if the airline also leaves the third seat in the row empty.
» Eat healthily. He recommends separating proteins and carbohydrates by at least three hours, especially when eating rich restaurant food.
» Order the fish, it is likely to be local.
» Always ensure you get eight hours' sleep. You and your business will suffer otherwise.
» When arriving in a new city, you can get to know it quickly by hiring a cab driver to take you around it for a couple of hours.
» Rather than having to take a laptop everywhere, use software such as PCAnywhere or AT&T's VNC, which allows you remote control access to your home computer from, for example, an Internet café.[6]

KEY LESSONS

» The telephone is not a substitute for face-to-face communication.
» It is important to remain objective and look at things from an outsider's perspective.
» Take care of your health by eating carefully and getting enough sleep.

SUSAN BONHAM: A CULTURAL CHAMELEON

Susan Bonham[7] was born in Moscow to Russian and Czech parents. She lived in Prague between the ages of 4 and 16 and then in Hamburg and Israel. After her marriage she moved to Canada where she worked in television and as a teacher of German; then back to Israel where she taught English; to the US where she worked as a freelance editor; and finally to the UK, where she has lived with her husband and three children since 1993.

Bonham speaks six languages. When asked which language she thinks in, she replies, "I think in whichever language I'm speaking at the time, that's the trick."

Global words

Bonham now writes journalism and fiction, with a book of short stories and a novel to her credit. She also used to edit a literary magazine, where she made the decision to assemble an international editorial board with representatives from Europe, the US, and Israel. She was based in London but was in continual communication by e-mail, phone, and fax with the board and the magazine's contributors, who came from all over the world, from as far apart as Sri Lanka and Russia.

In Bonham's opinion having such a global input gave the magazine a special kind of color. To her, it was fascinating to discover how people in other countries thought and interesting that they felt getting published in the UK was so valuable. "The distance was irrelevant, we could still communicate," she comments. "It was no different to them being on the other side of London."

One interesting assignment was as an investigative journalist writing a long piece about something that happened during the Second World War. In her research she had to travel a great deal, to Germany, Switzerland and Israel, and to communicate with many people in the US. Each contact she made led to ten or so others all over the place, and she could not have managed to cover the ground she did, either physically or virtually, without e-mail and her cellphone. It helped that she could speak their languages and that she was prepared to speak to them at any time of day or night, so that the time difference was not a problem.

Crossing cultures

Bonham's first book was about women living in foreign countries. She explains: "It was my way of thinking about people's experience of living 'abroad' – written as fiction, but based on how I have observed a lot of women behaving in real life." The book was set in many different countries, and it was frustrating to Bonham when a German producer who had optioned it to turn it into a feature film tried to twist everything so that it was based in or somehow connected to Germany. "This was trying to make it fit another culture and didn't reflect the spirit in which it was written," she comments. In contrast, when working with a film company in Hollywood on a film of the investigative piece she had written, they had no problem with the different cultural backgrounds, they just wanted the story as it really happened.

Bonham remarks that some places she had lived didn't feel permanent – "they were just transitions" – but that others, like Israel, New York, and London, did seem like home. "I'm a bit of a chameleon," she laughed. "If I feel comfortable in a place I can be very much of a local patriot."[8]

KEY LESSONS
» Diversity in people and attitudes is a valuable asset.
» Time differences need not be a problem with the latest kinds of communication.
» Flexibility and adaptability help you fit in.

NOTES

1 Gibson, Rowan (1996) *Rethinking the Future*, Nicholas Brealey Publishing, London.
2 Source: Author's interview with Rowan Gibson; www.rethinking group.com.
3 Source: Author's interview with Mike Garbe.
4 Marx, Elisabeth (2000) *Breaking through Culture Shock*, Nicholas Brealey Publishing, London.
5 Source: Author's interview with Elisabeth Marx.
6 Source: Author's interview with Michael Lissack; www.lissack.com.
7 Name changed at her request.
8 Source: Author's interview with Susan Bonham.

Key Concepts and Thinkers

This chapter looks at the key theories and theorists on working globally. It considers:

» what makes a successful global manager;
» defining culture shock;
» avoiding economy class syndrome;
» working in global teams;
» language issues;
» negotiating globally;
» Geert Hofstede;
» Fons Trompenaars.

CHARACTERISTICS OF SUCCESSFUL GLOBAL MANAGERS

What makes for personal and business effectiveness when working globally? A study of Fortune 500 firms[1] revealed that global leaders needed a core of characteristics, which were inquisitiveness, emotional connection, integrity, capacity for managing uncertainty, ability to balance tensions, business savvy (recognition of worldwide market opportunities), and organizational savvy (intimate knowledge of their firm's capabilities). The survey's authors commented:

> "Based on our interviews, the consensus was that global leaders are born and then made ... Global leaders, like great musicians or athletes, need superior talent, abundant opportunity, and excellent education and training to succeed."[2]

A McKinsey study of 59 senior multinational managers in China found that the following attributes characterized successful expatriates: optimism, drive, adaptability, foresight, experience, resilience, sensitivity, organization.[3]

Richard Lewis, author of *When Cultures Collide*, has the following list of what he calls "weapons for empathy" for a global manager, based on "accepting differences and building on these in a positive manner": tact, humor, sensitivity, flexibility, compromise, politeness, calm, warmth, patience, preparedness for discussion, will to clarify objectives, observation of other side's protocol, care to avoid irritants, careful listening, respect of confidentiality, inspiration of trust, constantly trying to see things from the other's (cultural) point of view.[4]

Fons Trompenaars, a noted author on cultural diversity, claims in *Riding the Waves of Culture* that the ability to learn from one's mistakes is perhaps the most important attribute when working globally:

> "Other cultures are strange, ambiguous, even shocking to us. It is unavoidable that we will make mistakes in dealing with them and feel muddled and confused. The real issue is how quickly we are prepared to learn from mistakes and how bravely we struggle to understand a game in which 'perfect scores' are an illusion, and

where reconciliation only comes after a difficult passage through alien territory. We need a certain amount of humility and a sense of humour to discover cultures other than our own: a readiness to enter a room in the dark and stumble over unfamiliar furniture until the pain in our shins reminds us where things are."[5]

CULTURE SHOCK

Most people experience "culture shock" when coming face to face with another culture or country for the first time (see Chapter 6 for advice on how to cope). There are various definitions of culture shock, a term introduced in 1960 by anthropologist Kalvero Oberg,[6] who saw it as having four phases.

» The "honeymoon," with emphasis on the initial reactions of euphoria, enchantment, fascination, and enthusiasm.
» The crisis, characterized by feelings of inadequacy, frustration, anxiety, and anger.
» The recovery, including crisis resolution and culture learning.
» Adjustment, reflecting enjoyment of and functional competence in the new environment.[7]

Elisabeth Marx prefers to see it as a triangle with three levels.

» "Emotions – coping with mood swings.
» Thinking – understanding foreign colleagues.
» Social skills and identity – developing a social and professional network and effective social skills."

The three sides of the culture shock triangle lead to the following areas where people should aim to become more effective when working globally.

» "Coping with the stress of the transition (achieving contentment).
» Changing the perception and interpretation of events and behavior (developing a way of thinking that is culturally effective).
» Developing better social skills and an international identity."[8]

Psychologists Colleen Ward, Stephen Bochner and Adrian Furnham, authors of *The Psychology of Culture Shock*, propose "the ABC model of culture shock" with three components, affect, behavior and cognitions, "that is, how people feel, behave, think and perceive when exposed to second-culture influences."[9]

» The affective component includes responses such as confusion, anxiety, disorientation, suspicion, bewilderment, perplexity and "an intense desire to be elsewhere."
» The behavioral component addresses the idea that "the rules, conventions and assumptions that regulate interpersonal interactions, including both verbal and non-verbal communication, vary across cultures." Culturally inappropriate behavior may lead to misunderstanding and cause offense.
» The cognitive component considers shared meanings, what people see as "established verities" which do in fact vary across cultures. "For instance, when persons from a male-dominated culture find themselves in a society that practices gender equality, the conflict between these two irreconcilable positions . . . affects how the participants see each other, how they regard themselves, and whether either party will be influenced to change their views as a consequence of the contact."[10]

Sensitivity training, "emphasising the cultural relativity of most values, the advantages of cultural diversity, the validity of all cultural systems and tolerance of ambiguity," is beneficial in giving people the skills and information to help them deal effectively with culture shock.[11]

Robin Pascoe, author of *Homeward Bound: A Spouse's Guide to Repatriation*, defines reverse culture shock, or what he calls "re-entry shock," as "simply the shock of being home. It's the reverse culture shock you experience in your own country when you visit places that should be familiar to you, but aren't; try to interact with people you should feel comfortable with, but don't; or face situations you should be able to handle, but can't."[12] He claims that this can be worse than adjusting to a new culture, and that the effects can last up to two years.

ECONOMY CLASS SYNDROME

One well-publicized danger of air travel is deep vein thrombosis (DVT), often called "economy class syndrome" although it can happen to passengers sitting anywhere in the plane – a recent victim was former US Vice President Dan Quayle who became ill after a busy round of air travel and who was presumably not flying economy class.[13] Passengers on long-haul flights are most at risk; a flight of less than two hours may be risk-free *unless* it is after another flight of two or more hours or you have spent two hours seated while waiting to take off.

To reduce your risk of DVT, follow the following advice:[14]

» Don't wear anything that impedes your circulation.
» Flex your calf muscles frequently (see www.airhealth.org for exercises).
» Don't sleep for more than two hours.
» Avoid sitting with your legs crossed for more than a few minutes at a time.
» If you are in a high-risk group (if you have a family history of blood clots, are obese, are a woman taking the contraceptive pill, have diabetes, heart disease or cancer, have had a recent injury or surgery or are over 60), talk to your doctor about taking anticoagulants or wearing medical compression stockings (available from www.ecs-dvt.com).

GLOBAL TEAMS

An article in the *McKinsey Quarterly* gives some examples of the breadth of situations in which teams may need to work together across the world:

"Software developers in the United States and Europe work with programmers in India to design systems and write code; bankers trade a common book of US government bonds around the world 24 hours a day; medical specialists collaborate with local doctors in remote regions to diagnose and treat rare conditions; and country managers coordinate production plans and marketing campaigns across Europe."[15]

Managing and working in teams comprised of members from different countries and cultures present many challenges. The concepts of teamwork and leadership vary from culture to culture, for example, and this can lead to misunderstanding. Time differences can also be problematic – even though communication by e-mail is obviously possible, it is not possible for teams whose members are in the Far East and the US to talk on the phone during normal working hours. It is also difficult when team members do not physically meet to develop the kind of trust and mutual credibility that is necessary if they are to achieve their task quickly and effectively.

An executive from a multinational company provides some instances of the effects of not managing global teams well:

> "In my company, we are having great difficulties with such groups. We've had strategic plans suffer and careers derail because of complications arising from multinational groups. Just last month we killed a global product development project because the team had taken so long that the competition had already sewn up the market."[16]

Lionel Laroche, president of cross-cultural training company ITAP Canada, explains the sources of miscommunication in international teams:

> » "Differences in body language or gestures ... For example, Bulgarians shake their heads up and down to mean no. In addition, the way people count on their fingers is not universal: the Chinese count from one to ten on one hand, and eight is displayed by extending the thumb and the finger next to it. The same gesture is interpreted as meaning two in France and as pointing a gun in North America.
> » Different meanings for the same word ... The French word *char* means army tank in France and car in Quebec ... While North American executives talk about 'exciting challenges' repeatedly, British executives use this word to describe only children's activities.
> » Different assumptions made in the same situation ... For example, although the sight of a black cat is considered a lucky event in Britain, it is considered unlucky in many other countries. Dragons are viewed positively in China, but negatively in Europe and North America."[17]

In order to avoid misunderstandings and to make sure that everyone is "singing from the same hymn sheet," it is important to take the time to clarify instructions and summarize the decisions made. It is also important for everyone to use language that is as simple as possible, particularly if the communication is in writing and there is no chance to check that everyone has understood.

Jon Katzenbach and Douglas Smith, authors of *The Wisdom of Teams*, suggest four basic elements that global teams require if they are to work successfully together, regardless of geographic location and cultural identity.

» The team must have complementary skills that will enable them to achieve their task.
» Goals must be established, together with individual and group accountability for their achievement.
» There must be an agreed common approach to getting the work done.
» The team needs to have a common purpose that makes the work worth the effort.[18]

HOFSTEDE, GEERT

Dutch social scientist Dr Geert Hofstede is director (emeritus) of the Institute for Research on Intercultural Cooperation (IRIC), an independent research institute in the Netherlands that he co-founded in 1980. He conducted one of the most famous surveys into cross-cultural issues, at multinational giant IBM in 1968 and 1972. This generated data from 40 countries and 50,000 respondents, and was published in the international bestseller *Culture's Consequences*.[19]

Hofstede's research focused on differences in national culture at the individual and organizational level and on their implications for management and policy making. According to Hofstede, culture is made up of elements in four categories:

» *Symbols* – "words, objects and gestures which derive their meaning from convention." Examples are language, modes of address, dress codes, and status symbols.
» *Heroes* – "real or imaginary people, dead or alive, who serve as models for behavior within a culture."

» *Rituals* – "collective activities that are technically superfluous but, within a particular culture, socially essential," such as celebrations, meetings, writing memos, planning systems.
» *Values* – "broad feelings, often unconscious and not open to discussion, about what is good and what is bad, clean or dirty, beautiful or ugly, rational or irrational, normal or abnormal, natural or paradoxical, decent or indecent."[20]

National culture differences can be classified according to five dimensions, the first four derived from the IBM survey, the fifth from research by Michael Bond at the Chinese University of Hong Kong. These are:

» *Power distance* – "the degree of inequality among people which the population of a country considers as normal: from relatively equal to extremely unequal."
» *Individualism* – "the degree to which people in a country have learned to act as individuals rather than as members of cohesive groups: from collectivist to individualist."
» *Masculinity* – "the degree to which 'masculine' values like assertiveness, performance, success and competition prevail over 'feminine' values like the quality of life, maintaining warm personal relationships, service, caring, and solidarity: from tender to tough."
» *Uncertainty avoidance* – "the degree to which people in a country prefer structured over unstructured situations: from relatively flexible to extremely rigid."
» *Long-term orientation (LTO)* – compared to short-term orientation. "Values positive rated in LTO are thrift and perseverance; values negatively rated are respect for tradition, and fulfilling social expectations, 'keeping up with the Joneses'."[21]

IRIC (http://cwis.kub.nl/~fsw_2/iric) provides the Value Survey Module (VSM), a questionnaire enabling researchers to measure the five Hofstede dimensions. It has a sister organization, ITIM (www.itim.org), which carries out training and management consultancy based on IRIC's research.

LANGUAGE

How much does the ability to speak more than one language help you in working globally? Learning a foreign language is difficult for many people, particularly adults, and the smattering of language skills that is all many acquire at school will not get them very far when they are trying to do business in another country.

There are some who claim that English is really the world's - or certainly Europe's - *lingua franca*. For example, an article in *Business Week* notes:

> "English is firmly entrenched nearly everywhere as the international language of business, finance, and technology. But in Europe, it's spreading far beyond the elites. Indeed, English is becoming the binding agent of a continent, linking Finns to French and Portuguese as they move toward political and economic integration ... Everyone in the corporate food chain is feeling the pressure to learn a common tongue as companies globalize and democratize."[22]

The number of English speakers throughout the world is said to exceed the population of China, and English is an official language in more than 75 countries.[23] Caroline Moore, a linguist with the British Council, explains: "As people interact with more people in different ways, they need a language in common. And in many countries, to be seen as a player, you need English."[24]

Telecommunications companies Alcatel (France) and Nokia (Finland) both use English as their corporate language, as does pharmaceutical company Aventis, the result of a merger between France's Rhône Poulenc and Germany's Hoechst. At CERN, the European Laboratory for Particle Physics in Switzerland, scientists from 82 countries do business in English.[25] The Internet, as well as the globalization of business, is ensuring that English is widespread outside Europe as well, being an official language in Singapore and India and a sought-after skill in countries across Africa and Asia.[26]

The apparent dominance of English notwithstanding, some fluency in the language of the country in which you are working is still a very desirable asset, if only because it makes it easier to form relationships with your colleagues and they will tend to react more favorably towards you. Knowing something of a language also helps you appreciate the country's culture and heritage, and making the effort to speak is evidence of some respect for those with whom you are working.

NEGOTIATION

As we have seen, cultural differences often create problems in communication and this can become particularly evident in negotiations. This reaches down to the deep level of the expectations that people have of others' behavior and the basic assumptions they make about what a certain action or decision means, which vary from culture to culture. Nevertheless, global managers are estimated to spend more than half their time in negotiations and this is one of the most important skills for them to possess.[27]

Richard Lewis, author of *When Cultures Collide*, gives some examples:

» "Americans are deal-oriented, as they see it as a present opportunity which must be seized ... For the Japanese, the current project or proposal is a trivial item in comparison with the momentous decision they have to make about whether or not to enter into a lasting business relationship."

» "French, Spaniards, most Latin-Americans and Japanese regard a negotiation as a social ceremony to which are attached important considerations of venue, participants, hospitality and protocol, timescale, courtesy of discussion and the ultimate significance of the session. Americans, Australians, Britons and Scandinavians have a much more pragmatic view and are less impacted by the social aspects of business meetings."

» "For the Americans, time is money and they wish to compress as much action and decision making as possible into the hours available ... The Germans will place emphasis on thoroughness, punctuality and meeting deadlines ... The French give pride of place to logic and rational argument ... The British also give priority to quiet reasonable, diplomatic discussion."[28]

Based on a study of the cultural differences of negotiators from the US and Japan, Richard Menger of St Mary's University, Texas, makes the following recommendations:

"One implication is that members of negotiating teams should study the other team's culture to gain a better understanding

and appreciation of the perspectives from which they are negotiating. Achieving cross-cultural understanding may be especially
critical in terms of each culture's perspectives on information
sharing, individualism versus collectivism, and hierarchy versus
egalitarianism."[29]

TROMPENAARS, FONS

Fons Trompenaars is managing director of Trompenaars Hampden-
Turner Intercultural Management Consulting in the Netherlands
(www.7d-culture.com). Author or co-author of bestselling books such
as *Riding the Waves of Culture*, *Seven Cultures of Capitalism*
and *21 Leaders for the 21st Century*, he has conducted 15 years
of research into cross-cultural differences and worked for Royal
Dutch/Shell handling operations in nine different countries.

Trompenaars carried out a study in 15 countries based on a questionnaire measuring cultural differences by searching for shared sets of
basic assumptions as distinctive characteristics of different cultures. The
database currently contains the results of more than 55,000 responses.
From this developed the Seven Dimensions of Culture Model, a frame-
work to help managers structure their experiences of doing business
and managing across cultures.

Trompenaars compares culture to an onion, with layers that can be
peeled off. The three layers of culture are as follows:

» "The outer layer ... the visual reality of behavior, clothes, food,
language, housing, etc. This is the level of explicit culture."
» "The middle layer refers to the norms and values which a community
holds: what is considered right and wrong (norms) or good and bad
(values)."
» "The inner layer is the deepest: the level of implicit culture ...
The core consists of basic assumptions, series of rules and methods
that a society has developed to deal with the regular problems
that it faces. These methods of problem-solving have become so
basic that, like breathing, we no longer think about how we do
it. For an outsider these basic assumptions are very difficult to
recognize."[30]

Each of the seven cultural dimensions is like a continuum between two contrasting basic values. The dimensions are:

» *Universalism vs particularism* – what is more important, rules or relationships?
» *Individualism vs communitarianism* – do we function in a group or as an individual?
» *Specific vs diffuse cultures* – how far do we get involved?
» *Affective vs neutral cultures* – do we display our emotions?
» *Achievement vs ascription* – do we have to prove ourselves to receive status or is it given to us?
» *Sequential vs synchronic cultures* – do we do things one at a time or several things at once?
» *Internal vs external control* – do we control our environment or work with it?[31]

Mapping cultural characteristics along these dimensions can help recognize, respect and reconcile cultural differences.

NOTES

1 Gregersen, Hal, Morrison, Allen and Black, J. Stewart (1998) "Developing leaders for the global frontier", *Sloan Management Review*, Fall.
2 *Ibid*.
3 "Survey of 50 senior Western multinational managers in China", McKinsey Shanghai office, 1997.
4 Lewis, Richard D. (2000) *When Cultures Collide: Managing Successfully Across Cultures*, Nicholas Brealey Publishing, London.
5 Trompenaars, Fons (1993) *Riding the Waves of Culture: Understanding Cultural Diversity in Business*, Nicholas Brealey Publishing, London.
6 Oberg, K. (1960) "Cultural shock: adjustment to new cultural environments", *Practical Anthropology*, 7, 177–82.
7 Ward, Colleen, Bochner, Stephen and Furnham, Adrian (2001) *The Psychology of Culture Shock*, Routledge, Hove.

8 Marx, Elisabeth (2000) *Breaking through Culture Shock*, Nicholas Brealey Publishing, London.

9 Ward, Colleen, Bochner, Stephen and Furnham, Adrian (2001) *The Psychology of Culture Shock*, Routledge, London.

10 *Ibid*.

11 *Ibid*.

12 Quoted in Pascoe, Robin (2000) "Going home", FT.com, October 27.

13 Conlon, Michael (2001) "Away on business", *Reuters Business Report*, August 23.

14 www.airhealth.org.

15 Benson-Armer, Richard and Hsieh, Tsun-Yan (1997) "Teamwork across time and space", *McKinsey Quarterly*, 4, 18–27.

16 Hambrick, Donald C. (1998) "When groups consist of multiple nationalities: towards a new understanding of the implications", *Organization Studies*, Spring.

17 Laroche, Lionel (1998) "Managing cross-cultural differences in international projects", *Engineering Dimensions*, November/December.

18 Katzenbach, Jon R. and Smith, Douglas K. (1998) *The Wisdom of Teams*, McGraw-Hill, Maidenhead.

19 Hofstede, Geert (1980; revd edn 2001) *Culture's Consequences: International Differences in Work-Related Values*, Sage, Beverly Hills, CA.

20 Hofstede, Geert (1994) "Business cultures", *Little India*, September 30.

21 *Ibid*.

22 Baker, Stephen, Resch, Inka, Carlisle, Kate and Schmidt, Katharine A. (2001) "The great English divide", *Business Week*, August 13.

23 Anthony, Ted (2000) "A global language is hailed", *Washington Times*, May 22.

24 *Ibid*.

25 Baker, Stephen, Resch, Inka, Carlisle, Kate and Schmidt, Katharine A. (2001) "The great English divide", *Business Week*, August 13.

26 Anthony, Ted (2000) "A global language is hailed", *Washington Times*, May 22.
27 George, Jennifer M., Jones, Gareth R. and Gonzalez, Jorge A. (1998) "The role of affect in cross-cultural negotiations", *Journal of International Business Studies*, 29, December, 749–51.
28 Lewis, Richard D. (2000) *When Cultures Collide: Managing Successfully Across Cultures*, Nicholas Brealey Publishing, London.
29 Menger, Richard (1999) "Research briefs: Japanese and American negotiators: overcoming cultural barriers to understanding", *Academy of Management Executive*, 13, November, 100–101.
30 www.7d-culture.com/cont11a.htm.
31 *Ibid*.

Resources

This chapter provides sources of advice and information, ranging from books on cross-cultural issues and working in other countries, to Websites on:

- » cross-cultural training;
- » general information;
- » health;
- » Internet telephony;
- » jobs and careers;
- » networking;
- » relocation;
- » translation.

CROSS-CULTURAL PREPARATION AND TRAINING

www.7d-culture.com

Trompenaars Hampden-Turner Intercultural Management Consulting, founded by Fons Trompenaars and Charles Hampden-Turner, provides consulting, training, publications, and computer-based learning resources that "aim to improve the global effectiveness of organizations by providing solutions that reconcile cultural differences through best practice." The consultancy has a network of specialists across the world and has formed an alliance with KPMG management consulting.

www.berlitz.com

As well as its language training in 35 countries, Berlitz offers cross-cultural orientation programs for business travelers, expatriates and their families. The courses cover daily life, social and business dos and don'ts, how to communicate and negotiate across cultures, and managing people from other countries. There is repatriation adjustment training, for example fitting in again at work, finding an appropriate position, and personal and family concerns. In addition, Berlitz provides global business training for those working globally without actually relocating, incorporating geography, politics, economics, social life, history; management, decision making, organization and planning, leadership communication; boss–subordinate and client–supplier relationships; verbal and non-verbal communication; negotiation styles; and work styles compared with local business practices.

www.cultureshockconsulting.com

This Website gives details of cross-cultural programs and seminars from the publishers of the Culture Shock! guides. Courses offered include country briefings, managing multicultural teams, selling overseas, customer care skills, Internet, e-mail and cross-cultural communication skills, repatriation, presentations and writing across cultures, and assessment programs.

www.itim.org

Geert Hofstede's training and management consultancy in the Netherlands, ITIM, specializes in national and organizational culture and its impact on business. The services offered include helping with handling diversity in people, markets, motivations and management styles, and creating unity and effective cooperation within an organization.

www.peoplegoingglobal.com

People Going Global are communications consultants specializing in cross-cultural training. They are based in Washington DC, but this site gives detailed information on cross-cultural issues faced when living and working in Australia, Austria, Britain, Canada, China, Denmark, Finland, France, Germany, India, Italy, Japan, Mexico, the Netherlands, New Zealand, Russia, Singapore, South Africa, South Korea, Spain, Sweden, Switzerland, Thailand, Tonga, the UK and the US.

GENERAL INFORMATION

www.embassyworld.com

This site provides a directory and search engine of embassies and consulates throughout the world, as well as links to international telephone directories and information on visa requirements.

www.escapeartist.com

This site, based around the *Escape from America* magazine, provides a fascinating insight into different lifestyles and offshore opportunities. The site includes information on living overseas, country profiles, sources of reference, advice on investing offshore, and international marketplaces for real estate and jobs. The emphasis is more on alternative lifestyles than mainstream business.

http://expat.ft.com/expat

FT Expat is an extensive information site for expatriates and those working abroad. There are sections with articles on health, property, tax and law, travel, international investment, personal finance and *FT Expat* magazine. Links are provided to offshore funds and shopping sites.

www.getcustoms.com

Getting Through Customs (GTC) is a software, training and research firm for international travelers. Its Website offers information on more than 65 countries worldwide, including business practices, protocol, a cultural overview, cognitive styles, religious and social influences on business, and gift-giving services as well as more general data such as travel, medical and historical information. There is also a holiday and time zone guide, articles on cultural differences and "Cultural IQ" quizzes.

www.gksoft.com/govt/

This site gives details of governments on the WWW, a database of governmental institutions, including parliaments, ministries, offices, law courts, embassies, city councils, public broadcasting corporations, central banks, political parties and multi-governmental institutions. There are entries from more than 220 countries and territories.

www.going-there.com

This is a subscription-based online and face-to-face relocation service currently covering Brussels, Dublin, Frankfurt, Geneva, London, Moscow, Paris and Prague, with Amsterdam, Milan, Hong Kong and Mexico City to come. A global network of researchers, expatriates and editors provide the answers to practical questions and can offer a person-to-person briefing in the destination city from an insider's perspective. There is a recommended list of suppliers in each city and advice for partners and families, as well as online communities and language guides. Subscriptions start from $1,250.

www.worldbiz.com

Worldbiz.com is a site from International Cultural Enterprises, Inc., offering guides written by US executives on doing business in various countries, with topics such as greetings and introductions, names and titles, etiquette, developing relationships, business dress, exchanging favors, being on time, communication style, negotiating, gift giving, business entertainment and useful addresses. The guides are delivered by e-mail after payment online and countries covered include Algeria,

Bahrain, Cambodia, Denmark, Egypt, France, Guatemala, Hong Kong, Ireland, Japan, Kenya, Lebanon, Mauritius, Nepal, Oman, Philippines, Qatar, Russia, Sri Lanka, Turkey, Ukraine, Venezuela and Yemen.

www.wtgonline.com

This site provides extensive information based on Columbus Publishing's *World Travel Guide* that claims to cover every country in the world, available in Dutch, English, French, German, and Spanish. There is additional information on various cities and airports (www.worldairportguide.com). City or country travel guides can be downloaded to a handheld computer or personal digital assistant. For each country it incorporates general information such as maps; population and geography; climate; history and government; public holidays; passport/visa requirements; duty free; money; health; travel, international and internal; accommodation; social profile; business profile; sports and activities; regions and cities.

HEALTH

www.cdc.gov/travel/

This site offers health advice from the US National Center for Infectious Diseases on specific destinations, including links to reference material, information on current outbreaks, vaccination recommendations, and advice for special needs travelers.

www.doh.gov.uk/traveladvice/index.htm

This site offers travel health advice from the UK Department of Health, including immunizations, eating and drinking safely, major diseases and the precautions to take, and the latest health updates.

www.travhealth.com

Personal medical services are provided in eight languages for travelers and expatriates, enabling users to store all their medical data in one place. There is a specific questionnaire for families with children, as well as additional packs for gynecology and obstetrics, cardiovascular care and sports injuries. TravHealth manages the service for its subscribers but has no access to the actual medical information.

www.tripprep.com

Travel Health Online is a site offered by Shoreland, a provider of information for travel health professionals. There is destination information on all countries, from Afghanistan to Zimbabwe, information on illnesses from altitude sickness to yellow fever, and details of travel medicine providers worldwide.

INTERNET TELEPHONY

www.deltathree.com

A PC-to-Phone dialer,iConnectHere offers PC-to-Phone calls to anywhere in the world from as little as 1.9 cents per minute. It is currently only available for the PC.

www.dialpad.com

This is a PC-to-Phone service for both PC and Mac users. Calls to over 200 countries, including mobile phones, with prepaid plans are available.

www.net2phone.com

Net2Phone offers PC-to-Phone, PC-to-Fax and voice mail services for the PC. Calls can be made from your computer to any phone in the world for as little as 4 cents per minute.

JOBS AND CAREERS

www.elance.com

This site is an extensive freelance professional marketplace. The "service providers" (freelancers) create a profile for each of their skills, bid for projects and then pay eLance a 10% transaction fee for each successful bid. Buyers post projects for free. Billing and payment is handled by eLance. The site covers accounting and finance, administrative support, business strategy, graphic design and multimedia, legal, software and technology, web design and development, writing and translation, project management and sales.

www.ework.com

The freelance marketplace eWork Exchange has over 300,000 users who complete skills profiles (listing one is free) and then search and bid for projects.

www.expatnetwork.com

Based in the UK, Expatnetwork offers a range of employment-related services, as well as a comprehensive online resource for expatriates, including country profiles, healthcare, shopping, travel services, and members' forums. There is a jobsearch database for overseas jobs, a candidate register to advertise your CV to employers, automatic e-mail notification of new jobs, company profiles, contract advice and news, and a CV service.

www.freelancesearch.com

This is a freelance jobs site and directory specializing in writers, editors, proofreaders, and translators.

www.freelanceworkexchange.com

A freelance marketplace where project listings are free and members pay a monthly fee to access the site. There is also advice on managing a freelance business.

www.globalcareercenter.com

A site offering international jobs, currently in 57 countries around the world. There is a resumé database and a job "agent" to search for suitable jobs and e-mail you when a new one is posted.

www.gojobsite.com

A searchable job site covering France, Germany, Ireland, Italy, Spain, and the UK. Consistently voted the number one site in independent performance surveys of online recruitment, GoJobsite has received investment from Manpower Inc., which is represented on the board, so it can draw on the experience of a traditional recruitment company. It covers 35 sectors and in September 2001 advertised over 275,000 vacancies.

www.jobpilot.com

A "career market" covering Austria, Belgium, Czech Republic, Denmark, France, Germany, Hungary, Italy, the Netherlands, Norway, Poland, Spain, Sweden, Switzerland, the UK, the US, the Middle East, Australia, Hong Kong, India, Korea, Malaysia, Singapore, and Thailand. Jobpilot is based in Germany and offers more than 100,000 positions each day. There is a resumé database and links to advice on relocation, as well as services for recruiters such as online assessment.

www.monster.com

Monster.com is a global career portal, consisting of local language sites in Australia, Belgium, Canada, France, Germany, Hong Kong, India, Ireland, Italy, Luxembourg, the Netherlands, New Zealand, Singapore, Spain, the UK, and the US. It connects job seekers and employers via job postings and a searchable database of resumés. As at September 2001 the network had 11 million job seeker accounts and over 19 million visits a month. There are also chat rooms and message boards, as well as advice on job seeking and career management, a site specifically for senior executives (www.chiefmonster.com) and Monster Talent Market for contract workers.

www.stepstone.com

This is a career portal operating in 17 European countries plus India and a pan-European section. In the first six months of 2001 StepStone had more than 25 million user sessions and it had more than a million registered subscribers and over 100,000 job listings. The site offers a resumé database, job matching and e-mail notification of new listings, as well as category and free text searching of the job database. StepStone also provides a candidate sifting tool for recruiters, using a structured online questionnaire to matched defined competencies in multiple languages.

NETWORKING

www.backtomyroots.com

A global community for expatriates and exchange students that offers local and international information and resources, as well as providing the opportunity for members to create a personalized home page with only the information they want, find other expatriates, join in online discussions and upload photographs to a password-protected page so they can be shared with friends and family.

www.expatboards.com

This site provides discussion boards, classified advertisements and resources for expatriates, mainly in Europe, which seem to be well visited.

www.expatexchange.com

Based in the US, this site is an online community for English-speaking expatriates. There are over 140 country and topic networks as well as resources and advice on relocation and living abroad, and a weekly e-mail newsletter.

www.expatica.com

This is an active networking and information site for English-speaking expatriates in Belgium, Germany, France, and the Netherlands. There is also a jobs marketplace and a section for HR professionals. The individual country sites feature local, international, and business news, advice on relocation and housing, what's on listings, shopping, eating and drinking, groups and clubs, classified advertisements, and discussion forums.

www.liveabroad.com

The Network for Living Abroad (outside the US, that is) provides a newsletter, Website and message boards for expatriates around the world. Associate members can post messages free of charge; full members get free advice, newsletters and special rates on books about overseas life.

www.womanabroad.com

This is a networking site and magazine for women expatriates, offering news, articles, members' advertisements, jobs and advice.

RELOCATION ASSISTANCE

www.directmoving.com

This is a worldwide relocation portal offering resources and information related to relocation, available in English, French, and Spanish. The site covers countries and cities, hotels and travel, jobs and careers, home search, language and culture, moving your goods, health and insurance, and expat kids. There are also various relocation tools, including cost of living and salary comparisons, a currency converter and a home space planner. A directory contains details of more than 10,000 relocation specialists worldwide.

www.monstermoving.com

An offshoot of the monster.com career Website, monstermoving.com began by offering relocation information for more than 1,500 cities in the US, but after acquiring international relocation consultancy Craighead Inc. has expanded to offer advice on Australia, Belgium, Brazil, Canada, China, France, Germany, Japan, Singapore, and the UK. There is extensive coverage of such subjects as business style, social life, healthcare, types of housing, schools, transport, the banking system, weather forecasts, and the expatriate community.

www.overseasjobs.com

International job opportunities for professionals, expatriates and what the site calls "adventure seekers" are provided. This is part of the AboutJobs.com network, which includes SummerJobs.com, Resort-Jobs.com and InternJobs.com. Services offered include a keyword search for jobs, e-mail notification of new postings, and advice on resumés. The site is developing a resumé database facility.

TRANSLATION SERVICES

http://world.altavista.com/sites/gben/pos/babelfish/trns

AltaVista has a free online translation service based on Systran software. About 150 words or a Web page can be translated from English into French, German, Italian, Portuguese, Spanish, Japanese, Korean, and Chinese and vice versa; from German into French and the reverse; and from Russian into English. Be aware that the translation is somewhat basic, will not handle technical terms, and is intended to convey the general sense of the document rather than a perfect piece of prose.

www.freetranslation.com

A site that boasts fast translation but only of the gist of a text, not word for word. Translate from English to Spanish, French, German, Italian, Norwegian, and Portuguese, and from Spanish, French, German, and Portuguese to English. The site also offers fee-based professional translations at various levels.

www.systranet.com

Systran, developers of the software that underlies many of the translation Websites, offers free online machine translation of users' files between English, French, German, Italian, Portuguese, and Spanish. There is also a fee-based human translation service in association with Berlitz and a dynamic translation service for Websites.

http://dictionaries.travlang.com

Free online translating dictionaries from Afrikaans, Czech, Danish, Dutch, Esperanto, Finnish, French, Frisian, German, Hungarian, Italian, Latin, Norwegian, Polish, Portuguese, Spanish, Swedish and Turkish into a variety of languages. For example, there are dictionaries from Portuguese into Dutch, English, Esperanto, French, German, Italian, Spanish and Swedish and vice versa. The site also offers a free multilingual dictionary program for Windows, which rather oddly translates between two natural languages by using Esperanto as an intermediate language.

www.worldlingo.com

Free online machine translation from English, Chinese, French, German, Italian, Japanese, Korean, Portuguese, Russian, and Spanish into English, Chinese, Dutch, French, German, Italian, Japanese, Korean, Portuguese, and Spanish. WorldLingo also offers instant quotes for professional translation by native speakers of over 40 languages, including Website and software localization. It also provides a fee-based service for multilingual online chat in ten languages, where you write a message in your language and your chat partner instantly sees the message in both your language and theirs.

BOOKS

The following books and series are useful guides to various aspects of working globally and cross-cultural issues.

» Hofstede, Geert (2001) *Culture's Consequences: Comparing Values, Behaviors, Institutions and Organizations across Nations*, Sage, Beverly Hills, CA. An updated and expanded edition of Hofstede's classic guide to diagnosing and comparing cultures and the implications of cross-cultural issues for management, based on a wide-ranging study at IBM.

» Hofstede, Geert (1994) *Cultures and Organizations: Software of the Mind*, HarperCollins, London. An exploration of differences in the way strategists think and why there is confrontation between people, groups and countries. The book offers practical solutions for dealing with conflict between different groups in business.

» Trompenaars, Fons and Hampden-Turner, Charles (1997) *Riding the Waves of Culture: Understanding Cultural Diversity in Business,* Nicholas Brealey Publishing, London. Based on research involving thousands of people in 50 countries, this book explores the five key factors affecting how people deal with each other, together with the cultural dimensions of our attitude to time and nature. There are examples and case studies of how to respect and reconcile different cultures.

» Hampden-Turner, Charles and Trompenaars, Fons (2000) *Building Cross-Cultural Competence: How to Create Wealth from Conflicting Values,* John Wiley, Chichester. Building on the dimensions of culture identified in *Riding the Waves of Culture*, this book explores the proposition that "foreign cultures are not arbitrarily or randomly different from one another. They are instead mirror images of one another's values, reversals of the order and sequence of looking and learning" (p. 1).

» Trompenaars, Fons and Hampden-Turner, Charles (2001) *21 Leaders for the 21st Century: How 21 World-Class Leaders Are Shaping the New World of Business*, Capstone Publishing, Oxford. Examples of how intercultural dilemmas affect leadership and how successful leaders exhibit transcultural competence and are able to create strategies that integrate the dilemmas.

» Marx, Elisabeth (2001) *Breaking through Culture Shock: What You Need to Succeed in International Business,* Nicholas Brealey Publishing, London. This book explains the "culture shock triangle" and is full of examples of how international executives are working successfully in other countries. There is advice on living overseas, helping children adapt, relocation checklists, medical issues, and returning home.

» Axtell, Roger (1997) *Gestures: The Dos and Taboos of Body Language around the World*, John Wiley, Chichester. Descriptions of over 200 gestures – greetings, beckonings, farewells, terms of endearment, insults – used in 82 countries, which may help avoid an embarrassing *faux pas*.

» Lewis, Richard D. (1999) *When Cultures Collide: Managing Successfully across Cultures*, Nicholas Brealey Publishing, London. A guide to working and communicating across cultures, giving both general and detailed advice on etiquette, body language, and negotiating in a wide range of different cultures.

» Culture Shock! series. Culture Shock Consulting produces guides to various countries' customers, traditions, social and business etiquette. Countries and areas covered are Argentina, Australia, Austria, Belgium, Bolivia, Borneo, Britain, California, Canada, Chile, China, Cuba, Czech Republic, Denmark, Ecuador, Egypt, France, Finland, Germany, Greece, Hong Kong, Hungary, India, Indonesia, Iran, Ireland, Israel, Italy, Japan, Korea, Laos, Malaysia, Mauritius, Mexico, Morocco, Myanmar, Nepal, Netherlands, Norway, Pakistan, Philippines, Scotland, Singapore, South Africa, Spain, Sri Lanka,

Sweden, Switzerland, Syria, Taiwan, Thailand, Turkey, Ukraine, United Arab Emirates, USA, Venezuela, and Vietnam.

» Kogan Page "Doing Business" series. Kogan Page publishes guides to various aspects of conducting business in and with selected countries, including Azerbaijan, the Baltic States, Bulgaria, China, Croatia, the Czech Republic, Egypt, France, Georgia, Germany, Hungary, India, Japan, Kazakhstan, Kuwait, Latin America, Libya, Poland, Romania, Russia, Saudi Arabia, South Africa, Spain, Turkey, the Ukraine, the United Arab Emirates, and Uzbekistan.

Ten Steps to Making it Work

Ten steps to working globally successfully:

1 Be curious about other cultures
2 Research, research, research
3 Get advice
4 Find yourself a mentor
5 Network
6 Keep all your paperwork in order
7 Take care of your health
8 Update your skills
9 Be realistic with yourself
10 Above all, enjoy the experience.

1. BE CURIOUS ABOUT OTHER CULTURES

Perhaps the most important criterion for working globally is being curious about other people and how they live and work. This is not something that should wait until you are about to start a foreign assignment – the most successful international operators are those who have been genuinely interested in other countries and different cultures since their student days and often before.

You can learn about another culture by reading what experts have to say about its people and their behavior. However, there is really no substitute for a natural curiosity and developing an ability to observe and notice what other people do. A willingness to be adaptable and flexible will also help you fit in.

Small changes can make all the difference. For example, American expatriate Leon Chester became aware that his French colleagues greeted each other every morning with the traditional "ça va?," a handshake and a short conversation. "So, after a while, I just started walking about shaking hands with 100 people every morning," he said. "It was obvious that this small gesture made a great difference – it made people feel cared for."[1]

Along with a willingness to watch and learn goes humility. There is a tendency for MBA-educated Western executives to assume that they "know it all," but local business practices and expertise can be just as powerful. Value differences instead of seeing them as negative aspects. Continually remind yourself to keep an open mind and it will become second nature to absorb valuable information and insights from those around you.

2. RESEARCH, RESEARCH, RESEARCH

Doing as much research as possible before you arrive in a foreign country can help ease the transition and give you confidence that the venture will succeed. Be sure to use information from more than one source, to avoid taking on someone else's attitudes or prejudices.

The kind of areas you need to find out about include the following:

» The country itself, its areas, cities, history, religions, politics etc.
» Requirements for work and residence visas, particularly for your partner if you have one.

» Housing costs and availability, including which areas it is best to live in and whether there are any expatriate "enclaves."

» Don't neglect finding out about the minutiae of everyday life. Knowing what to do when you need to post a letter, what time the shops are open and what you can expect in terms of banking or transport, for example, can help relieve the worst and most unsettling effects of culture shock.

» If you have a partner, what are the social and employment opportunities for them?

» If you have children, is the local schooling of a good standard or do you need to investigate international schools? For younger children, in some countries the proportion of women who work is lower than in others, so daycare may not be readily available and could well be more expensive than you are used to. Also, in a country such as France where daycare is state run, you may not have access to it.

» Can you take your pet(s)?

» What is the crime rate – violent crime is high in US; in France car theft and burglary are the most common types of crime. In South American countries such as Brazil, there is a risk of children being kidnapped for ransom. If you are going to be in a very poor country and therefore relatively rich by local standards, security may be a particular problem.

» Don't forget to find out whether your Internet service provider has an access number from your destination, or whether you need to find a local provider. You may want to obtain a Web-based e-mail address (such as those available from Hotmail or Excite) so that you can pick up your e-mail from anywhere, including a cybercafé.

3. GET ADVICE

There are some areas in which it is best to obtain professional advice, to forestall any later problems:

» Tax can be a particularly complex area, both for expatriates and for those who are working on short-term assignments. Consult a good tax adviser about the best way to minimize the total tax paid and avoiding paying tax in more than one jurisdiction, if possible.

» Make sure that you are fully aware of the requirements for residence, immigration, and work permits. If in any doubt, get advice.

» Consult an insurance adviser about both general and medical insurance that is suitable for the country in which you are going to be living, or blanket coverage if you are a frequent traveler.

» Establish the best banking arrangements for you – you may need a local bank account and credit card, or you may be able to keep your home-country bank, perhaps using Internet banking to manage the accounts. Find out how much money you can take into and out of the country.

» Don't forget about your pension. Depending on your home-country regulations, you may not be able to pay into a pension account if you have no income there, so you may need to investigate alternative arrangements.

4. FIND YOURSELF A MENTOR

Having a mentor with experience of the culture to which you are going can make a tremendous difference. Mentors have been defined as "seasoned individuals who support, guide, and provide counsel to less experienced colleagues in order to facilitate their careers."[2] They can be used before an expatriate leaves on an assignment, while they are abroad, and after they have returned home. Mentors are also useful as advisers to those managing global teams, for example, or needing to negotiate with people from other cultures.

Nancy Mueller, author of *Work Worldwide*, compares a mentor to a role model but says that it takes the concept a stage further: "Here you establish a definite association with an experienced and trusted advisor . . . Mentoring goes well beyond answering a few questions and directing you to others. A mentor takes a personal, vested interest in helping you succeed."[3]

She recommends discussing the following questions before making a final selection of mentor:

» "Has the person 'been there and done that'? Was he or she successful in doing what you want to do?"

» "Is the person accessible and willing and able to invest time and energy in your relationship?"

» "What do you want and expect from the mentoring relationship? What does the potential mentor expect from you in return?"

» "How often will you get together and by what means? Do you want to meet only occasionally or at regularly set times? Maybe you can't meet with your mentor in person because of geographical distance. If so, it's important to establish a nurturing relationship through regular contact by phone or by e-mail."[4]

What should your mentor be able to do for you? They can assist you with finding a job abroad in the first place. They can help make sure that your expectations about your work overseas are realistic and that you are not demanding too much of yourself. They can warn you about some of the problems you are likely to encounter, and suggest solutions when you do come across a difficulty.[5] They can provide an objective sounding board to give you the perspective you need.[6]

5. NETWORK

Networking is a vital skill when working globally, for both expatriates and those operating internationally from their home base. In many cases it may well be your contacts that lead to the job in the first place, and having a wide social circle can provide ready sources of advice, information, and support.

Expatriate clubs, particularly women's groups, frequently have orientation programs or welcome networks for those new to the area. Embassies and consulates can usually provide information on local expatriate clubs. If you have children attending an international school, there may be a parent association. Other ways of meeting people include sport and health and fitness clubs, religious activities or doing volunteer work for local charities.

If you want or need to network to improve your career prospects, or if you are freelance and your job depends on contacts, Donna Messer of ConnectUs Communications Canada offers the following guidelines for networking:

1 *Be prepared*. Have business cards, a profile of who you are and a professional picture for use in directories etc.

2 *Be open minded.* Be friendly when meeting other people and listen carefully to what they have to say. You never know who might have the potential to help you.

3 *Don't be afraid to ask.* Be sure about what you need and who you want to meet, but also be clear about what you have to offer and who you know.

4 *Give without expectation.* Introduce yourself to as many people as possible and ask how you can help them. Building relationships will help you find common interests.

5 *Set realistic and achievable goals.* To help you achieve them, connect with people in relevant organizations and associations.

6 *Think laterally.* Ask questions that will give you a more in-depth picture of everyone you meet and give them a chance to talk about themselves, which will help you identify the right people for you.

7 *Self-promote.* Understand your features and strengths and be prepared to talk about them effectively.

8 *Communicate.* Smile, make eye contact, introduce yourself. Be articulate and enthusiastic. Don't forget that listening is as important as speaking.

9 *Organize.* Having good records of who you have met and how they can help you will save you time in the long run.

10 *Teamwork.* If you think of yourself and the people you meet as being part of a team, you will all be working together to build better relationships.[7]

6. KEEP ALL YOUR PAPERWORK IN ORDER

If you are able to lay your hands easily on the necessary paperwork, it can help ease the impending sense of crisis when you have a problem, which always seems magnified and more significant when you are outside your home country. The kind of detail you need to have available includes the following.

» Photocopies of the relevant pages of each family member's passport.
» Passport-sized photographs of each family member.
» Birth certificates and any other relevant papers, such as marriage, adoption or naturalization certificates.
» Wills and telephone number of solicitor.

» Medical insurance details and medical and dental records, if available.
» Insurance certificates for property and motor vehicles.
» Driver's licenses.
» Lease or rental agreement for housing, if appropriate.
» Employment contracts, if appropriate.
» Bank account and credit card numbers, together with relevant telephone numbers in case of theft or loss.

7. TAKE CARE OF YOUR HEALTH

There are two aspects to living healthily when working globally: ensuring that you take all necessary precautions for the country in which you are living, and maintaining a beneficial lifestyle as a frequent traveler. You also need to make sure that you have adequate travel and medical insurance that is applicable to the country or countries you will be visiting.

If you are going to live in another country, talk to your doctor well before you go and arrange for the necessary vaccinations. Some vaccines require you to have more than one dose and do not become effective for a number of weeks. Without an International Certificate of Vaccination for diseases such as yellow fever, you may be denied entry to certain countries. You may also need to find out about prevention strategies for insect-borne diseases such as malaria and Japanese encephalitis.[8]

It may well be worth considering a full medical before you leave your home country, particularly if your family is going with you or if you are going to a developing country. Make sure that you have sufficient health insurance and that you know the location of a doctor who speaks your language, if one is available. Also establish whether it is a good idea to take a comprehensive first-aid kit with you, including syringes, and a medical reference book. A dental check-up is advisable, since standards of dental care vary across the world.

If you or someone in your family has an existing medical condition, find out the generic rather than trade names of any prescription drugs they have to take so that you will be able to obtain them when abroad. And if you have a serious allergy, wear a medical bracelet or necklace, perhaps with information translated into the language of your destination.

You will be able to obtain a list of local doctors who speak your language from your embassy or consulate.

As a frequent flyer you are at risk of different ailments. According to US sleep research consultancy Alertness Solutions, the effects of frequent business travel include memory loss, mood swings, attention lapses, loss of vigilance, lower reaction time, and poorer decision making.[9] And a detailed clinical study sponsored by the World Bank found that significantly more health insurance claims were filed by employees who traveled, and that frequent travelers account for three times as many claims for the treatment of stress, anxiety, depression, and other psychological-adjustment disorders as non-travelers.[10]

While it is not always easy or possible for busy executives to take time off to recover from a business trip, allowing sufficient time to catch up with the work that is waiting for you when you return is one way of reducing the stress. Making sure you take sufficient exercise and watching your diet will also help.

8. UPDATE YOUR SKILLS

Before you begin working globally, you may want to invest in some cross-cultural training, particularly if you are going to be working with a culture where the rules are somewhat different to your own. Beena Rajendra, a cross-cultural trainer, explains: "When you're doing business and you don't know the so-called expectations of your client group, your business can be doomed. You need a code-breaker to understand what the other person is saying."[11]

For example, problems can even arise over something as apparently simple as giving a present: "What you give a client as a gift, what colours a present is wrapped in, when and how it is given, can make or break a business relationship."[12]

Or take the example of John Lema, an IT professional for a US company that was building an online grocery system in Hong Kong and Singapore. He found that he was unaware of how to ask questions in a way that would encourage his Asian team members to respond: "Everyone would just answer with a simple yes or no all the time," he said. "I had to learn to be extremely specific in what to ask ... Plus, culturally, my Asian co-workers weren't used to asking questions."[13]

You may also want to review your language skills, depending on where you are working. Chris Brewster, director of the Centre for European Human Resource Management at Cranfield University, comments, "You can manage quite well without language skills, but if you've got them, your position in the employment market is so much stronger."[14]

Helen Vandevelde, a writer on recruitment issues, outlines the skills that will help maintain an individual's value in the global economy:

"The key talents are flexibility to adapt to different tasks, the ability to locate sources of knowledge quickly and screen out superfluous information, versatility in responding to changing circumstances, the ability to anticipate difficulties and resolve them speedily, and managing relationships with team colleagues."[15]

Of course, being in a foreign environment, even if you are plunged in at the deep end, will offer you many opportunities to hone your skills and become a more globally competent person.

9. BE REALISTIC WITH YOURSELF

It is a cliché but nevertheless true that unless you know yourself you won't be able to really get to know anyone else. The people who are most successful working globally are those who have strong self-knowledge and a solid sense of their own values, ethics, strengths, weaknesses and expectations, while being able to respect differences in others. If you know that you are the kind of person who finds it difficult to adapt and are not particularly gregarious, then you may not be ideally suited to working globally.

Be sure of what you are hoping to gain from your experience of working globally and what you are prepared to commit – and maybe even sacrifice – to make it work. Realistic expectations will give you a foundation on which to build and make the most of the opportunities.

And don't be too hard on yourself. After the initial problems of culture shock, if you are struggling, ask other people in a similar situation how they felt and seek help if you think you need it, from your company if you have one or perhaps from a counseling service.

If things really aren't working even after you have given your best, don't be too proud to admit that the assignment is wrong for you. Some

25% of expatriate postings fail, so you wouldn't be alone. It is far better to cut your losses and find a more rewarding job or assignment than to risk long-term emotional or psychological damage.

10. ABOVE ALL, ENJOY THE EXPERIENCE

Working and living abroad gives you exposure to new ways of thinking about the world and different sets of values. If you approach it with an open mind and take full advantage of the opportunities and the challenges, it may well lead to significant personal growth for you as well.

Working globally gives you access to a whole new set of friends, many of whom will remain in contact with you. It also gives you real experience of other countries and their people, more vivid and wide-ranging than you are able to obtain as a tourist. It is an experience that most treasure and few forget.

NOTES

1 Postelnicu, Andrei (2000) "Xenophobes need not apply", *Financial Times*, June 28.

2 Kram, K.E. (1985) *Mentoring at Work*, Scott Foresman, Glenview, IL.

3 Mueller, Nancy (2000) *Work Worldwide: International Career Strategies for the Adventurous Job Seeker*, John Muir Publications, Emeryville, CA.

4 *Ibid*.

5 Ward, Colleen, Bochner, Stephen and Furnham, Adrian (2001) *The Psychology of Culture Shock*, Routledge, Hove.

6 Lefko, Mark (2001) "It's lonely at the top – who do you turn to?", *Los Angeles Business Journal*, August 27.

7 Messer, Donna (2001) "Building business internationally", *Woman Abroad*, September, p. 13.

8 Armenia-Cope, Robin (1995) "Protecting employee health during travel abroad", *Managing Office Technology*, August 1.

9 Reported in Upton, Gillian (2000) "Hard landing for travellers", *Financial Times*, August 28.

10 Reported in "Heavy travel can hurt worker health, family", *Minneapolis Star Tribune*, May 15, 2000.

11 Bain, Jennifer (1999) "How to do business in a diverse world", *Toronto Star*, August 4.

12 *Ibid*.

13 Jana, Reena (2000) "Doing a double take", *InfoWorld*, February 14.

14 Vandevelde, Helen (1999) "How to win in a global economy", *Daily Telegraph*, February 18.

15 *Ibid*.

Frequently Asked Questions (FAQs)

Q1: What kind of people work globally and why?

A: See Chapter 2.

Q2: How has the development of communication influenced global work?

A: See Chapters 3 and 4.

Q3: How do people working globally use the Internet?

A: See Chapter 4.

Q4: How can I find a job overseas?

A: See Chapter 4.

Q5: Is globalization a good thing?

A: See Chapter 5.

Q6: What kind of training do I need to work globally?

A: See Chapter 6.

Q7: What is culture shock and what can be done to ease it?

A: See Chapters 6 and 8.

Q8: What makes a successful global manager?

A: See Chapter 8.

Q9: Who are the main thinkers on cross-cultural issues?

A: See Chapter 8.

Q10: Where can I find more information about working globally?

A: See Chapter 9.

Acknowledgments

I would like to thank all those who have talked to me and given me information about their experiences and their companies. In particular, thanks are due to Susan Bonham, Mike Dolan, Mike Garbe, Rowan Gibson, Michael Lissack and Elisabeth Marx. I am also grateful to my publishers, Mark Allin and Richard Burton, for their patience and encouragement.

Personal thanks go to Jon Lansdell, Melanie Byng, Kate Santon and Sue Hunter for always being there to listen; to my parents and their partners, Janet and Jim, Frank and Alison, for their continual support; to my daughters, Jasmine and Cassie, for being very patient, making innumerable cups of coffee and always loving me; and to Jack, for making my world a better place to be.

Index